TRIUMPH THROUGH FAILURE

Triumph through Failure

A Theology of the Cross

John Navone, S.J.

WIPF & STOCK · Eugene, Oregon

Wipf and Stock Publishers
199 W 8th Ave, Suite 3
Eugene, OR 97401

Triumph Through Failure
A Theology of the Cross
By Navone, John J, SJ
Copyright©1984 by Navone, John J, SJ
ISBN 13: 978-1-62564-964-5
Publication date 11/1/2014
Previously published by St. Paul Publications, 1984

Dedicated to:

James G. Powers, S.J., Robert J. Spitzer, S.J.
Bernard J. Tyrrell, S.J.

CONTENTS

PREFACE

Of the many forms of failure, whether culpable or not, death is the one form that everyone must endure. Poverty, hunger, violence, war, oppression of conscience, lack of freedom in professing one's convictions, impositions by powerful political minorities and by totalitarian states with all the aberrations and injustices that follow, are all certain facts of human failure which we must inevitably confront.[1]

We confront failure on all levels of our humanity. There is failure in the use of the gifts of the earth, the unlimited exercise of intelligence, and enjoyment of freedom, and in the acceptance of the call of an infinite God. The failure to achieve fulfilment at any one of these levels may contribute to a particular frustration that may destroy the wholesome harmony necessary for happiness.

Failure to have necessary sustenance for the body, to have food, shelter, or physical security may lead to illness or even death. Failure to enjoy a freedom of the spirit to reflect, to raise questions and to seek answers, may lead to the death of the spirit. There is no authentically human life when the human spirit is held captive by ideologies and structures which do not allow the intelligence to function fully.

There is the failure of persons to reach fulfilment when they are not allowed to choose their own values, when decisions are forced upon them. The *Gulag Archipelago* by Solzhenitsyn reveals the fate of millions who are victims of a modern form of slavery. There is failure when men are condemned to try to find their fulfilment in their world only, when they are denied the opportunity to hear the revealed truth about the final purpose of life. Failure always implies that there are persons who do not benefit at some levels of their existence from the sources of life as they should. They are failing to reach fulfilment. Failure at any level of human need impairs human wholeness.

The Good News of God's compassionate love in Jesus Christ and his Holy Spirit expresses the Church's mission and message. God's compassionate love in Jesus Christ, the foundational experience of the Christian Church, reaches out to human suffering and failure at every level of our individual and social experience and takes as many forms as there are needs to be met. The story of God's compassionate love in Jesus Christ reminds Christian faith that such love can go unrecognised, can be rejected, can meet with a failure in effecting the good that it intends. Nevertheless, the experience of God's compassionate love in Jesus Christ and his Holy Spirit grounds the Christian conviction that, however we may fail to reciprocate, God's love towards us is unfailing and unqualified by our personal or social merits. The unconditional love of God for us is symbolised by the Cross. We are loved even as sinners and enemies and fools. We are summoned by this love to become friends, to learn to love as God has loved us in Jesus Christ and continues to love us in his Holy Spirit. The experience of the Christian community confirms that the learning process is not without many failures, whether culpable or not. Self-deception and group-deception is always a possibility; the authenticity of our love or righteousness is never to be taken for granted. The truly religious person *seeks* the Kingdom of God and his righteousness; the self-righteous or pseudo-religious person assumes that such righteousness is to be fully identified with himself, with his ideologies, values and desires. The truly religious person will be open to learning about the meaning of authentic righteousness from those who are outside the religious community; he does not set limits to the activity of God's love in human affairs and welcomes it wherever it may be discerned. The story of the Good Samaritan is Jesus' way of reminding us that the merciful love of God may be most profoundly experienced in our lives from the quarters where we least expect it.

10

The God which we proclaim as love in our experience of Jesus Christ and his Holy Spirit within the Christian community is love in and with and through the facing of the appalling facts of life. The way of God's compassionate love is revealed in the story which Jesus Christ's life tells as one of voluntary self-sacrificing love for others. The way of the Cross is meant to engender and share the very love which motivates its acceptance; the redemptive and compassionate love of God in Jesus reveals the specifically Christian way of learning to love. The authenticity of the Christian's response to love God above all else finds its measure in the deeds by which he follows Jesus in self-sacrificing love for the neighbour. Such love is foundational: the neighbour loved has been given a ground or basis for reciprocating love. The Cross symbolizes the way in which the divine lover and the human lover-in-the-making are to be one, so that each lives in the other.

In a period of utopian ideologies and theologies, this book may serve as a reminder that we do fail and that our faith does not promise that we shall not fail. Yet, in spite of all this, we are given something to hope for. In the end, we will all fail, except God; for there is nothing in this world that will satisfy us.

The New Testament originates in the foundational experience of the love of God in Jesus Christ and calls us to follow Jesus' way of the cross for the authentic fulfilment of our humanity; the intent of its witness to the love of God in Jesus Christ is directed toward our ongoing conversion. Under the concrete conditions of our existence the fulfilment of our humanity in the religious conversion, that is thematised under the rubric of our becoming disciples of Jesus, implies the solution to the problem of evil. The New Testament seeks to convince us of the meaning of God's love for us which Christian faith found incarnate in the life story of Jesus; it attempts to persuade us to accept and live out the values inherent in that meaning. With the construction of the dramatic narratives of the New Testament, the Christian imagination articulates the meaning of God's love for us in

Jesus' entire life story, death and resurrection. Moved by the foundational experience of God's love in Jesus Christ, by their experience of conversion and redemption, the New Testament authors enriched and reshaped their memories of Jesus' words and deeds with appropriate images drawn from the Hellenistic world and above all from the Old Testament. They employed the symbolic power of their images — the Messiah, the Suffering Servant, the Lord, the Son of God — to evoke the meaning of their experience of God's love incarnate in Jesus Christ and of its meaning for us. The imagination of faith provided a key instrument for articulating the meaning of the purifying, illuminating, and transforming mystery of God's love for us in Jesus Christ. It serves Christian faith by articulating what this love does and what it does not do, thereby educating as well as expressing faith. The foundational experience of God's love in Jesus Christ and his Holy Spirit must be cultivated; its fruitfulness will vary with the cultivation it has received. The New Testament writings are one of the many forms which the cultivation of the primordial conversion experience takes. If we can fall in love with God in conversion, we can also fall out of love with Him. The Parable of the Sower reminds us that the ground of human consciousness can all too easily become absorbed in outer cares, or distracted by pleasures, or hardened in waywardness. Priests and ministers, ascetics and mystics, seers and prophets, are professional cultivators. The Church is an institutional reality that diffuses and irradiates, as well as cultivates, the foundational experience of God's love in Jesus Christ and his Holy Spirit among us.

The Christian conversion experience inaugurates a new orientation of our basic self-other-world-God relationship, a new way of being in love with ourselves, others, the world, and God that is our response to God's love flooding our hearts through the Holy Spirit of Jesus Christ given to us. The foundational experience of this love involves a call to holiness and a conversion from waywardness, the objective expression of the same love whereby the Father sends the Son to us and reveals his love in the Son's life, crucifixion, death, and resurrection and in the gift of the Holy Spirit. The experience of this love constitutes the infra-structure which gives rise to the forms and structures of the Christian community: Scriptures, fellowship, service, liturgy. The love which gives rise to the Christian community is characterised by listening (*kerygma* and Good News), relating (*koinonia*), serving (*diakonia*), and celebrating (*eucharistia*). It is a grace or gift with an inner demand for concretization: love takes particular forms and shapes. Paul catalogues the harvest of the Holy Spirit: love, joy, peace, patience, kindness, goodness, fidelity, gentleness, and self-control (*Ga* 5:22).

Religious formalism, while adhering to the letter of the Church's laws and embracing its structures, often risks missing their meaning as expressions of and channels for the purifying, illuminating, and transforming love of God in Jesus Christ and his Holy Spirit among us. Adherence to the Church's forms and structures is not incompatible with our alienation from the gift of God's love which originally brought them into being. The gift of God's love, the foundational experience and infra-structure of Christian life, demands a daily responsiveness within the historical particularities of our environment. Fidelity to the grace and demand of this love is never to be taken for granted. The Church is the matrix in which we examine the quality of our fidelity to this love; it is the matrix for maturation in fidelity, for understanding and accepting its implications so that we may love the persons and things presented to us with a love that is ordered by the same love that summoned into existence the Church itself. The beginning of our conversion may occur suddenly; however, living it out runs into blocs, impediments, disorientation, and bewilderment. In this respect, the Church exists to provide the means for the cultivation and maturation of our foundational conversion experience. Its stable organization is meant to inspire and foster the personal and social transformation of its foundational conversion experience; it is meant to help us cope with obstacles to the conversion process, with elements that devaluate, distort, water down, or corrupt it. Our selective inattention, or our failure to understand, or our undetected rationalization, are all elements which can impede the authentic living out of our foundational conversion experience.

13

We may be able to cite the last Council's documents, but one may doubt whether the home-fires are still burning. We need the fellowship of the Church as a matrix for working out an authentically Christian life.

Although this book makes no attempt to present a systematic theology of failure developed along the lines of a classical approach to theology, it does attempt to suggest major themes for such an approach. Reflections on the various levels of failure are enhanced by certain insights of non-ecclesiastical sciences. My reflections are based on the conviction that Christianity is the most instructive and stimulating explanation about the problem of human failure, one that really tells us most about what we can hope for, what we cannot.

The interest in the early Christian witness to Jesus lay in religious conversion. Christian preaching continues to proclaim religious conversion in terms of following Jesus Christ, his way of the cross, the way of unfailing love which reaches its culmination in the resurrection witnessed by the birth of the Church. Inasmuch as the way of Jesus is that of the Cross, the theological reflection of Christians cannot ignore the problem of failure, whether culpable or non-culpable.

Theology has been conceived as reflection on religion and in the present age as a highly differentiated and specialised reflection. In fact, Bernard Lonergan describes eight functional specialties in theology: research, interpretation, history, dialectic, foundations, doctrines, systematics and communications.[2] *Triumph through Failure* belongs to the eighth functional specialty, which Lonergan defines as follows:

> Communications is concerned with theology in its external relations. These are of three kinds. There are interdisciplinary relations with art, language, literature, and other religions, with the natural and the human sciences, with philosophy and history. Further, there are the transpositions that theological thought has to develop if religion is to retain its identity and yet, at the same time, find access into the minds and hearts of men of all

cultures and classes. Finally, there are the adaptations needed to make full and proper use of the diverse media of communication that are available at any place and time.[3]

Communication is a major concern, for it is in this final stage that theological reflection bears fruit. Without the first seven stages, of course, there is no fruit to be borne. But without the last, the first seven are in vain, for they fail to mature.

The Holy Spirit is where it acts. The Kingdom of God is where His Holy Spirit rules our hearts and minds. God is King where He effectively rules; and the meaning of his rule has been revealed to Christian faith in all the particulars of the story which Jesus Christ's life has told and continues to tell through the gift of his Holy Spirit in the Church. The love of God revealed in Jesus Crist and the gift of his Holy Spirit establishes itself in our hearts and minds as the rule or power of friendship: "No longer do I call you servants . . . But I have called you friends, because all things I have heard from my Father I have made known to you" (*Jn* 15:15). God rules all creation. All creatures are, willingly or unwillingly, his "servants"; however, the rule of his Kingdom to which his love in Jesus Christ summons us is that of the mutual presence, reciprocity, collaboration, intimacy and affection of friends. The Father's life is that of Jesus, a life he fully shares with his friends. Christianity proclaims that the friendships of men are the very means to the friendship with our God, for he who loves his neighbour has fulfilled the law. God sharing his heart and mind with us is the highest and most perfect act of friendship possible to us, his creatures; it is the fulfilment of every law, both human and divine, the ultimate perfection of that universe of persons God has called into being to become his friends (cf. *Rm* 8:28f):

> We know that by turning everything to their God co-operates with those who love him, with all those that he has called according to his purpose. They are the ones he chose specially long ago and intended to become true

images of his Son, so that his Son might be the eldest of many brothers.

The rule of God's friendship is realised to the extent that let God be the friend that He is, whether we experience him in the darkness as a transcendent Lover or in the light as an imminent Lover. These are the first two areas of religious experience described by Friedrich Heiler; the other five describe our experience of God as supreme beauty, truth, righteousness, goodness; as love, mercy, compassion; the way to him is repentance, self-denial, prayer; that the way is love of one's neighbour, even of one's enemies; that the way is love of God, so that happiness is envisioned as communion with him, or knowledge of him."[4]

The unfailing love of God, revealed in the life, death, and resurrection of Jesus Christ, summons all humankind to friendship; still, the summons can go unheeded. The story of Jesus is one of both acceptance and rejection. If authentic friendship with others can be evidence of our authentic friendship with God, the inability to be a true friend to anyone suggests a lack of friendship with God. Evidence of friendship with God is seen in our willingness to show compassion to those in need (1 *Jn* 3:17). By the same token, the lack of compassion for the suffering denotes the absence of God's rule of friendship in human hearts. Friendship can never be forced upon us. The love of friendship is always a free gift of oneself. Although Christianity proclaims that in Jesus Christ God is Love for us today and always, it also recognises the difficulty with which even Christians fully open themselves to this love. In Johannine teaching we are told that man turns away from this Love by centring his life and attention on himself, building on his weakness and mortality rather than on the creative power of God's love. The self-confidence of the world represents a radical turning away from God (e.g. *Jn* 15:5); the man who believes that he is self-sufficient independently of God's love walks in darkness (1 *Jn* 1:8; 2:2).

The first two chapters are a kind of statement of the question. The first chapter offers an overview of the various

16

levels of failure. The second chapter recognises the importance of the literary "sign of the times" as secular "parables" of failure.

The next three chapters focus on aspects of Jesus' relationship to failure, indicating how his freedom from the fear of failure reveals that unfailing Love which invests the human condition with its ultimate meaning and value.

The sixth and seventh chapters reflect on the social dimensions of failure, recognising that the Good News of the Gospel is for society, groups, structures, and the world.

The eighth and ninth chapters focus on the role of the Church in confronting failure. The Church's liturgical remembering gives expression to its ongoing foundational experience of God's love in Jesus Christ and his Holy Spirit, teaching us a way of remembering that is healing and creative of new possibilities for the future.

The tenth chapter focuses on the healing and liberating dimensions of the gift of God's love in Christ and his Church.

CHAPTER 1

FAILURE IN THE PERSPECTIVE OF FAITH

Failure, whether culpable or non-culpable, is a universal human experience. Death, the lot of all mankind, is apparently the ultimate failure. It raises the questions of God's existence, his goodness, and the possibility of an after-life; whatever the answers, death remains dreadful and communicates a terrible sense of failure. For Old Testament man, death was linked with every dimension and experience of failure, because failure was a kind of dying. For modern man, the experience of failure, whether culpable or not, still remains a kind of dying.

Jesus, like man in everything but sin, experienced human failure. He wept over Jerusalem which had not known the day of its visitation. His preaching failed to convert his people. His crucifixion was an act of rejection and public disgrace. The hatred vented upon him during his passion and death gave him a profound experience of moral evil. His last moments of life were filled with the consciousness of his failure to communicate his Father's message to his people. And when it was all over, his disciples realised that Jesus' acceptance of failure and death was the divinely appointed way for effectively communicating all that the Father wanted to communicate, even if Jesus himself might not have realised this in his final moments of consciousness.

The Church, the body of Christ, experiences failure. Vatican II startled people by admitting it. The *Pastoral Constitution on the Church in the Modern World* affirmed that the Church is painfully aware that among its clerical and lay members there has been infidelity to the Spirit of God during the course of many centuries. It affirmed that even today the Church is aware of how great a distance lies between the message it offers and the human failings of those to whom the Gospel is entrusted. The *Decree on Ecumenism* cited St John: "If we say that we have not sinned, we make him a liar, and his Word is not in us" (1 *Jn* 1:10). In this context the Church begged the pardon of God and of our separated brethren for its sins against Christian unity.

The End of Utopia

Today there is an over-riding awareness of failure pervading our social structures which have militated against social justice and civic concord, oppressing millions and impeding their human development. There is no corner of the globe where man has not, in varying degrees, experienced the failure of his social structures.

The failure of history to produce Utopia has disillusioned idealists of every era. Every age records its failures, its dramas of oppression, collective sufferings, deportations, massacres, and humiliations. Every age chronicles fresh social injustices, wars, greed and exploitation, in which man creates tragedy after tragedy for himself. The idea that there is to be a fulfilment *in* history, that the religious or social or political millennium will come in time, rather than at the end of time or outside of time, is debated. Regardless of the position taken in the debate, the fact remains that no age has been without a profound experience of historical failure. The historical process has not of itself produced peace and brotherhood among men. The apocalyptist's view of the human condition is one which implies the impossibility of human freedom and fulfilment within the historical process. Disappointment in the outcome of historical events leads to liberation from an illusion or self-deception that temporal beatitude constitutes salvation.

There is also a sense in which the future fails. Frequently man feels that he has no future, whether in his present historical situation or in terms of an after-life. To be without either kind of future indicates a state of oppression or destitution often found in contemporary literature and drama. Having nothing to remember implies having nothing to look forward to; on the other hand, an obsession with evil memories promises a future that is no future at all. The Church's remembrance of the transcending love of the cross empowers us with a future that transcends the ultimate failure of sin and death; remembering redemption redeems the future, transforming death into a transition in life rather than the ultimate failure of life.

Christians believe that Jesus is the image of God (e.g., 2 *Co* 4:4; *Col* 1:15), and that men bear his image, so that he stands no longer alone, but as the eldest of a large family of brothers (*Rm* 8:29). Jesus is the means by which the invisible God is revealed, the divine pattern on the basis of which man has been created. The historical Jesus is the image of God, the first of the new humanity that will share his imaging of God, and is already partially and inadequately adumbrated in Christians. The final destiny of mankind is that of being conformed to Jesus' image; it is a call which man can fail to answer by his failure to be human in terms of Jesus, the primal man, who is *the* image of God.

The failure to be human, to participate in the fullness of humanity embodied in Jesus, implies the rejection of true human existence, an existence which is divinely pre-programmed for the revelation of God through his image in the multiplicity of men who bear it throughout history. Failure to be an image of God implies a rejected gift, diminished existence, self untranscended, and self travestied into a counter-symbol of the glory of God which the self had been created to symbolize. To the extent that man fails to be the image of God, he falsifies himself, his true existence, his structured, pre-programmed being.

The Abba relationship, embodied in the historical Jesus, is the means by which God delivers and heals mankind. It is the divine response to ultimate human failure as symbolized by the Old Testament nexus of death and sin. Failure, whether culpable or inculpable, can always be redeemed into a kind of *felix*

21

culpa through the transforming power and meaning of love. This is the lesson of the cross, where the very symbol of failure and death has been transformed into a symbol of love and life. Love overcomes failure by reversing its meaning, by giving it a new meaning, a positive, redeeming meaning that becomes the message and good news of the disciples of Jesus.

Failure and Theophany

The meaning of things is a part of their reality. The meaning of Jesus' death, Christians believe, is different from that of any other death; it represents a unique reality. Because the meaning of a process is only fully understood in the term of that process, the meaning of Jesus' death is only grasped by the resurrection faith in which Jesus' death terminates. Jesus had attached a special meaning to his sufferings and death, as part of God's plan and purpose (*Lk* 9:22; 13:32; 18:31-33); they would have important results in which his disciples would share (*Lk* 22:15-20, 28-30). The disciples believed that this meaning explained their experience of the living Jesus after the death of the cross; hence, the reality of Jesus' death, as well as the reality of the suffering and failure that were intimately linked to it, is rooted in the meaning which Jesus had given it and which the disciples recalled. Failure, suffering, and death had been given new meaning; they had been transformed into a different kind of reality, a new reality, a healing and liberating reality.

Through the power and meaning of divine love, everything is a grace and works for our good; even failure, suffering, and death are endowed with the possibility of a theophanous quality that both illuminates and transforms the world. In fact, the wisdom of the cross suggests that perhaps the best way of enlightening and healing mankind is through the acceptance of failure, suffering, and death in the name of the absolute truth, love, and goodness of God. These are the effective means of the divine wisdom for the communication of that truth, love, and goodness which save the world by empowering it to transcend those evils which are genuinely lethal to the human spirit. Jesus accepts failure in his Father's name, and his Father accepts the failure of his Son because it is what his Son *is* that counts, rather than how he succeeds. Mankind is regenerated by this mutual acceptance of Father and Son through the medium of failure and death.

Although this book makes no attempt to present a systematic theology of failure, it does attempt to suggest major themes for such an approach. The non-Christian's experience of failure and suffering can contribute much to the Christian understanding of the same experience. The suffering of the six million Jewish martyrs and the struggles and suffering of Gandhi have much to tell us about the mystery of the cross, of the power communicated through the sufferings, failure, and death of the innocent.

An education which does not prepare youth to confront and endure failure is seriously deficient. Much of the power of Christianity derives from the wisdom of the cross regarding suffering, failure, and death. It is a realistic preparation for the inevitable experience of personal and social failure: "You will be hated by all men on account of my name" (*Mt* 10:22). No amount of wisdom or loving kindness can guarantee reciprocity; Jesus failed, and his authentic followers will also fail in this regard. In fact, Jesus assures them of their failure (*Mt* 24:9; *Mk* 13:13; *Lk* 6:22, 27; 21:17). They will be hated as the world hates Jesus (*Jn* 7:7; 15:18). Failure to win universal acceptance or even tolerance is the inevitable lot of the authentic disciple. Only he who can endure such failure will be saved: "The man who stands firm to the end will be saved" (*Mt* 10:22; 24:9). The endurance of failure in any of its many forms is a requisite for salvation; hence, authentic Christian discipleship is an education for failure.

The endurance of failure is not a passive posture; it requires, in its deepest Christian sense, an adherence to God, to truth, love, social justice and fraternity. Such adherence may provoke creative conflicts through which the ruth may be revealed and communicated in much suffering, conflicts aimed at the ultimate happiness and conversion of one's opponents. This was Gandhi's lesson. The willingness to endure suffering, failure, and death on behalf of truth was, for Gandhi, not only a test of one's authentic adherence to truth but also an indispensable means for the communication of truth, justice and fraternal love in society.

The cross is the greatness of God responding to the *felix culpa* of human failure. It also suggests that the greatness of the human spirit is measured in terms of a similar response to human and social failure, whether or not this failure be culpable. Failure is an invitation and a challenge to love. It is a cry for love epitomised by Jesus' agonised question: "My God, my God, why have you forsaken me?" The starving, rejected, humiliated, degraded, sick, invalids, and oppressed share in the cry of Calvary, "My God, my God, doesn't anyone love us?" Is there no love to respond to failure? Is there no compassion, no awareness, no concern? Does no one see or hear the misery of failure in its myriad agonising forms?

The resurrection of Jesus is the light after the darkness of failure; it is the Father's loving response to the cry of Jesus on Calvary. Wherever men throughout the world respond with genuine compassion to the anguish and misery of failure, the image of the Father's love shines forth, and a glimmer of what God is pierces through the darkness as a healing and merciful illumination. The Father's love is a response to the rejection and failure of his beloved Son on Calvary precisely because Jesus is his Son; the historical failure of Jesus to convert Israel does not alter the Father's love, but becomes the very means through which his salvation is accomplished and revealed. The Father loves his Son for what he is; he is like the father of the prodigal son whose love for his son does not cease at his son's failure. Human failure is the occasion when men discover whether anyone loves them; in this respect, it is perhaps the best test of love that man knows. From another point of view, our response to human failure reveals to us whether our love for others is genuine and, therefore, whether we share in the Father's love which raised Jesus from the dead and ultimately delivers all mankind from the conditions of death.

24

The cross raised the question of failure which the resurrection answered. God seemed to have failed Jesus. Jesus felt forsaken and was taunted by those who told him to come down from the cross if he was truly the Son of God. Jesus seemed to have failed his Father in not having converted Israel. Israel had apparently failed its God by not having accepted Jesus, his Word. The disciples also had failed their master by taking flight and, in Peter's case, by an express denial of association with Jesus. In fact, Jesus' failure seems so absolute that many scholars prefer to attribute Christianity to the creative power of St Paul rather than to Jesus himself. Jesus failed those who wanted a socio-political messiah. He did not liberate Palestine from Roman rule. The social, political, and economic structures of Palestine remained much the same as they had been the day of his birth; if anything, with the destruction of Jerusalem and the dispersion of the Jewish people, they became worse. Slavery, the condition of so many of the first Christians, remained a social constant for centuries. The first Christians were persecuted and martyred, sharing their Lord's suffering and death with its same power to communicate the truth, love, and compassion for human failure. St Stephen, the first martyr, echoed the prayer of Jesus on the cross that his executioners be forgiven because they did not know what they were doing. St Paul was among those executioners, and Stephen's prayer was effectively answered. The other martyrs revealed the powerful transforming effect and revealing character of their suffering and death, one with that of their Lord, when it was said that their blood had become the seed of Christians. Through their apparent failure, suffering, and death the effects of the resurrection were communicated for the regeneration of others. The effects of their suffering and death represented the term of a process which clarified the meaning of their sharing in the cross. They communicated, in union with their crucified Lord, a new life for others which represents a merciful healing of those whose sinful condition had been one of basic human failure. The resurrection of Jesus and the experience of its effects represent the Father's merciful and healing response to failure, suffering, and death; it is a response which has continued throughout history wherever failure, suffering, and even death are shared and transformed by love into the healing of ourselves and others.

Optimism and Christian Realism

Despite failure on its many levels, the Christian preserves a fundamental optimism towards the world; not the optimism of the agnostic humanist, but of the believer, who knows in faith that the world has been taken radically and irrevocably into the loving care of the Father through and with and in Christ. It is an optimism that endures in and through death, disaster and sin, because the Christian knows that it is in and through Christ's death that the power of his resurrection is communicated throughout the world. The Christian must be optimistic, then, but not utopian: optimistic because Christ has been raised from the dead as the first fruits of those who are subjected to God the Father; not utopian, not deluded into thinking that the inherent structures of the world can, of themselves, permanently bring peace and happiness.

Christian realism resists both the tendency to stress this-world values in such a way that the values of the world to come are neglected and the tendency to stress the values of the world to come in such a way that the values of this world are neglected. Either tendency not only excludes true values, but in doing so seriously distorts the values that are retained.[1] Pelagianism, an example of the first distortion, assumes that the mind and heart of man can achieve the triumph of the Kingdom of God in this world permanently by mere human means. It often takes the form of some earthly messianism which stresses the present and disregards the ultimate future. Quietism, the other extreme, is a failure to live up to the Christian vocation to use all the human means that learning and intelligence offer to create good social structures. The Christian seeks to avoid those two extremes of failure, doing everything or doing nothing, by relying on God's grace and contributing to the creation of a new world.

Christian realism recognizes that human failure which is sin has penetrated the world so deeply and has so weakened man that man cannot uphold and practise consistently his highest ideals without that healing of the mind and heart which is the gift of the Spirit. Although a utopian state of dedicated humanism is theoretically possible, there is no historical evidence for its sustained unselfish exercise in human history.

Triumph through Failure is concerned about present evils and the transformation of the world through the healing process of loving service. It affirms that by doing everything possible in the present to heal, enlighten and transform, the Christian is even now building up the everlasting Body of the Lord and hastening the day of final glorification and the coming of a new heaven and a new earth. It shares the concern expressed by Avery Dulles, S.J. in a book review that appeared in *Theological Studies* (1969, vol. 30, p. 124): "I wonder whether it is still adequate to recognise only the three standard sources of theology — Bible, monuments of tradition, and magisterial teaching. If it be true . . . that God speaks to us through secular history, it would seem to follow that the events and movements of secular history — and man's reaction to them in cultural expressions — should be reckoned as theological sources." The human anguish of failure takes on many forms in the secular history through which God speaks; it challenges everyone to a compassionate listening.

According to James Schall, the impatience of our times with our economic and political failures does witness to a greater glory.[2] The sense of urgency, the profound impatience with the failures of the secular order are not mere perversions. The theology of freedom means that there are important things to be done for man and by him. The urgency and the haste of the modern world are evident, but they are not enough of themselves. Schall believes that the urgency propounded by many economic and other specialists is very often intellectually but a thinly disguised effort to keep the *status quo*. Their visions are, all too often, too narrow for what in fact might come to be. As there is for man no love without a waiting, so there is no real progress without a gestation. We can believe that the

27

urgency is so great, that our problems are so enormous that only catastrophic failure lies ahead; nevertheless, we do not have to believe that the anguishes of today are prelude only to tragedy. Schall believes that the crisis of western civilisation and institutions, serious as it may seem, may be exactly what is required for the vision and hence the reality of a world much greater than our pessimistic social scientists, demographers, political activists, and theologians would lead us to believe. The waiting may well be the greater urgency. For it is the vision that shapes the reality, and our visions have been very narrow. Good will, passion, and feverish action do not suffice to preclude future failures. Schall believes that we can rush ahead and create another *novus ordo saeculorum,* but whose order will it be? Man needs to be saved from restricted visions, especially those that do not include the fact of an imperfect, fallible world. The assumption that the world *must* be perfect is often combined with the assumption that all disorder derives from exploitation and sin, so that it is a moral and political virtue to hate what is disordered or imperfect since it must be caused by evil, which we must hate in its representatives. Such visions allow no room for man in his finiteness, in his history, in his smallness, in his failures.

The Christian vision of failure in the world order and in the individuals who constitute it is that of its Lord who has revealed to us what it means to be moved by the love of God and neighbour. His creative vision accepted the fact of an imperfect, fallible world of finite men. He has embraced and elevated human finitude: "For it is not as if we had a high priest who was incapable of feeling our weakness with us; but we have one who has been tempted in every way that we are, though he is without sin. Let us be confident, then, in approaching the throne of grace, that we shall have mercy from him and find grace when we are in need of help" (*Heb* 4:15-16).

The vision of Christ overcomes the human failure to believe that man has nothing beyond himself, that his own values are merely what he creates for himself, that the social complexus of infinite relationships bear the ethical burden as substitute

28

for the person. The vision of Christ comprehends the finitude of human person and of human society. Christ the compassionate high priest "can sympathise with those who are ignorant or uncertain because he too lives in the limitations of weakness" (*Heb* 3:2). His vision counters that ideological perfectionist intolerance for allowing mistakes, that modern form of angelism which believes that this world can be paradise. It is embodied in a theological tradition where there is still room for those who hear the word but fail to practise it. They are called, especially by themselves, "sinners", and Christians are admonished to love them too somehow. This tradition counters the contemporary ideological mood where there seems no longer to be space for failures, where the problems confronting us are believed to be too vast, too pressing, to allow anyone the liberty to fail. It counters the ideologue's self-righteous assumption that "the others" have a monopoly on human failure. Christianity affirms that *all* men need Christ's redemption because *all* men fail. It affirms the validity of finite man, the man who is created by something other than himself, and its loyalty to the promise that will unite us, despite our many failures: "The one who guarantees these revelations repeats his promise: I shall indeed be with you soon. Amen: Come, Lord Jesus" (*Rv* 22:20).

CHAPTER 2

MODERN PARABLES OF FAILURE

The phenomenology of human failure, in its many dimensions and varieties, is dramatically present in the theatre. In fact, the theatre is among the most powerful means of communicating the meaning and impact of human failure. The theatre must be considered among "the signs of the times," containing the dreams of the times — some of the nightmares — to be scrutinised in the light of the Gospel to appreciate the relevance of the Gospel's healing and enlightening meaning and value for our contemporaries. The events of the theatre dramatically reflect the events taking place within ourselves, our contemporaries and our culture. They are literary events which often offer profound insight into our tragic flaws and those of our society; as such, they are among those "signs of the times" which Vatican II has called the Church to discern in the spirit of Christ (*Gaudium et Spes*, p. 11) and reflect the importance of literature affirmed by the same Council (*Gaudium et Spes*, p. 62).

If the theologian is not going to let the Gospel be shut up within the little church world, if he is convinced that it is something to be proclaimed to all men in their perennial quest for orientation in the complex field of social power and suffering, he will pay attention to the myths of the theatre, films, and literature. They represent the experiential matrix of faith, the experience itself from which believing arises. He will detect in these myths expressions both of that suffering which faith is meant to heal and articulations of that dream which faith is meant to realise. Through them he may attune him-

31

self better to the lives of his contemporaries whose journey to God must inevitably be travelled through a welter of personal affectivity.

The myths of drama are the dreams of the times which the theologian, like the Old Testament's Joseph in Egypt, must interpret. It is important that he discern what is of genuine value and what is specious, because the wrong dream may destroy a man and a society. Sometimes the dream is associated with sin and madness when a man, tragically deluded and mistaken about the meaning of his life, destroys himself in an attempt to force reality to conform to the shape of his illusions. There is a profound pathos in a man's (or society's) faithful response to a destructive illusion, to the wrong dream. Drama reveals much about man and the quality of his dreams; and the theologian is called to judge how man and his society can be transformed for better or for worse by them. Ultimately, the theologian will judge contemporary myths in the light of the Christian myth that stretches from creation to re-creation (Genesis to Apocalypse); for he believes there is no kind of experience that cannot be brought to judgment by this myth. Myth, in this case, implies truth, not falsehood; not primitive, naive misunderstanding but an insight more profound than scientific description and logical analysis can ever achieve. The language of myth in this sense is consciously inadequate, being simply the nearest we can come to a formulation of what we see very darkly.

The myths which the theologian must interpret and judge are a tissue of symbolism clothing a mystery. They reflect every man's odyssey through time in which he searches for answers to the mystery of his existence. Parallels have been noted between myths and dreams, in which myths have been seen as projections of, or objectifications of, man's inner strivings and desires. They tell us much about man's self-understanding and his groping toward an identity, about his bafflement and suffering. They tell us much about his experience of failure (whether culpable or not), of his inability to achieve his ideals and secure his future. The following plays offer some examples of the multiple dimensions of failure represented in modern drama.

32

Human failure pervades Chekhov's *Uncle Vanya,* wherein no one gets what he wants; no one changes his fortune. Chekov's people do not resolve their problems but have to go on more aware of them. Serebryakov does not get the estate or the money he wanted; Astrov goes on unable to love; Sonya does not marry the doctor; Yelena is not relieved of the boredom with her husband; Vanya still supports the despised professor. *Uncle Vanya* depicts failure in a story of missed opportunities. Each person ends more isolated than before in this comedy of inept people failing to achieve, of sensitive people surrounded by stupid ones, of good, selfless souls versus the self-centred. Some try to change the situation, but not with courageous dignity — yet with enough courage and dignity to be human and ludicrous. To a certain extent their failure implies pessimism, but as a life element within the comic. People must realise how bad their lives are before they will ever attempt to create other and better lives for themselves; nevertheless, Chekhov seems to realise that there are few men able to secure their perimeters and live without a sense of failure before what might have been.

In *The Skin of Our Teeth,* the modern everyman play by Thornton Wilder, failure is seen as intrinsic to the human condition. The Antrobus family is a symbol of the human race that time and again will narrowly escape all kinds of natural and self-willed calamities. It is mankind that from the beginning suffers from the heritage of failure, but forever attempts to rebuild the values it has destroyed. It is the family per se, with all their troubles, quarrels, and accidents, with their pride in what they have produced, their readiness to help those in distress, their inclination to fall victims to lust and power, their perplexity in the face of evil, their belief in spiritual values and their courage ever to begin anew after every failure that is truly the symbol of the human race.

The recognition of personal failure is the beginning of hope for a better life in William Inge's *Come Back, Little Sheba.* Lola, a perennial adolescent, wears a dreamlike expression and speaks to her husband like a little girl. She is lonely and spends her days doing nothing. Lola's immaturity leaves her unequipped to recognise her husband's problems and his grievances against her. She suffers intensely when he viciously berates her; nevertheless, it is precisely her capacity for such suffering that enables her to overcome her isolation from the adult demands of her domestic context. Through the intense suffering which has been inflicted upon her, Lola recognizes her failure and advances toward a deeper understanding and companionship with her husband. Suffering awakens her to his condition; it allows her to feel his need which calls out for her.

Impossible Integration

The failure to meet the challenge of one's social context is the theme of many plays. Blanche DuBois, in Tennessee Williams' *Streetcar Named Desire,* fails to come to grips with her social contexts, whether it be that of her past in Laurel, Mississippi, or that in the French Quarter of New Orleans. Both surroundings provide the strengths that overwhelm Blanche in her struggle for a respectable and peaceful human existence. Unable to face the problematic of either context, Blanche finally succumbs to a mental illness which isolates her from "harsh reality." She is too fragile, too sensitive, to resist the death-pull of sin and madness, of a world in conflict where "the animals inherit the earth."

In Ignazio Silone's play, *The Story of a Humble Christian,* which tells the story of the thirteenth-century Italian saint, who was elected pope, and took the name of Celestine V, it is rather the context that fails. Celestine concludes that the great organisation of the institutional Church is so powerful that it inevitably corrupts its administrators, and that genuine Christian witness is impossible in the office of pope. Celestine experiences a moral crisis which leads him to judge the historical structures of the papal government as no longer self-justifying; in fact, he finds them to be so seriously wanting and impervious to reform, the development of evolution, that his future vision of authentic Christian witness demands his resignation from office. His decision is a judgment about the failure of an historical governmental apparatus to respond to the then present need of the Christian community.

Arthur Miller's *The Death of a Salesman* is another play that indicts a certain kind of society for its failure to provide its members with a satisfactory vision of life. Willy Loman has the wrong dream and is destroyed by it. The "dream" is associated with the belief in untrammelled individualism and with the worship of success. Willy is profoundly incapable of warding off the shame and suffering that derive from a vision of life that he cannot make work. The competition of the business world is too much for him. He is incapable of the success he feels society demands of him. The pressures of a success oriented society, wherein respect must be constantly earned by endless achievements, eventually drive him out of his mind. In such a society, where respect is never gratuitously bestowed on anyone, failure is unbearable. To be successful comes to mean that a man is loved and approved; to fail is to find himself alone and not worthy of love and attention. The "phony dream" of success, the ideal of Willy's society, not only makes Willy peculiarly liable to suffering and eventually madness; it finally leads him to suicide.

Eugene O'Neill's plays abount in failures, wrecked existences haunted by feelings of guilt, alienated from what might be their natural surroundings and yet trying desperately to find some sort of sense or order or peace in their lives, if only for brief moments. *The Iceman Cometh* deals with the problem of aggregate failure in which the universality of loneliness among men tends to overshadow the suffering of individuals. The destitute outcasts who inhabit Harry Hope's bar attempt to escape from their oppressive sense of degradation and failure through dreams and drink. They display the irreconcilable contrast of man's yearning for a world of values, even illusory ones, with his incapacity to cast off whatever weight pulls him in the other direction. Dreams and drink are pseudo-solutions to critical human problems; they provide transient satisfaction and create an illusory self-substantiation. This is the story of man's aggregate failure to rise above transient satisfactions and to decide what is truly good for himself.

Homelessness is a dimension of human suffering and failure among those who seek a confirmation of their identity in environment. Homelessness reflects the suffering of those who cannot say: "I am because my fellow-citizens know me." The hunger for a home burns in the main characters of John Steinbeck's *Of Mice and Men,* a play which depicts the life of transient ranch hands. For them "home" is not the place where they live but the place where they lived as children. Steinbeck's Lennie and George dream of an earthly paradise where all men can achieve happiness and security. And it is the instinct, or universal drive, for such a "home" that Steinbeck dramatises in *Of Mice and Men* — together with its inevitable failure, a failure which is a part of humanity itself. Lennie is not a simple case of retarded development but rather a representation of the inarticulate and powerful yearning of all men for a "home". Lennie's innocent but destructive desire for pleasures ultimately becomes the means by which the Dream of Paradise (the farm) is destroyed. Only the ritual of mutual responsibility, the religion of the shared dream, enables man to transcend his own particular desires. When this ritual is destroyed, the dream is no longer attainable.

Man's inability to understand and cope with death is treated in Ionesco's theological nightmare, *The Killer.* Berenger, the protagonist, is an ordinary citizen anxious to help others. He finds himself in the City of Radiance wherein all is seeming perfection, a paradise whose architect is obviously meant to represent the almighty architect of the world. The city is almost deserted because a mysterious killer roams the streets. He takes the lives of many people and cannot be apprehended by the authorities, who accept his activities with fatal indifference. When Berenger tracks the killer down, he attempts to argue the case of humanity, but neither flattery, promises, concessions, nor threats are of any avail. The killer is unmoved by pity, vanity, reason. To each he replies with a cynical, absurd chuckle. Berenger tries desperately to convince him that murder is wrong and useless; he becomes engaged in a debate with his own mind, giving reasons pro and con, finding that if there is no reason to kill, there is also no logical reason not to kill. Finally, lost and in panic before the killer's menacing silence, he struggles for reasons beyond logic. Failing to understand the mysterious, he loses power over himself, drops his pistol, and is a victim of the killer's knife. Human reason fails to penetrate the mystery of death.

The failure of justice, democracy, and other human values, when money is God, is the subject of Friedrich Duerrenmatt's play, *The Visit of the Old Lady.* The town of Guellen boasts of its democratic heritage but is suffering from poverty and unemployment. Clara Wascher, now Madam Zachanassian, a multibillionaire, arrives as the only hope. Many years previously she had been forced to leave Guellen after her childhood sweetheart, Ill, had deserted her and their child. After taking up the life of a prostitute, she met the oil magnate Zachanassian and becomes the richest women in the world. At a ceremonial banquet, she offers a billion dollars in return for justice. She restages her trial, but all the original witnesses are in her employ. For reparations, she asks for the life of Ill. At first the citizens are horrified; however, as time passes they begin to have second thoughts about their refusal of her offer. Clara Zachanassian is prepared to wait and give the inhabitants a sample of what they could buy on credit. Knowing they have not the means of paying, Ill watches them all taking advantage of Clara's credit. With the town's new prosperity, Ill is now regarded as the guilty one, the sacrificial victim needed to cleanse the city. He is murdered by the entire community in a ritualistic ceremony. Clara drops the check for a billion at the feet of the mayor and boards the train as all the worshippers at the temple of money chant, "Long live her goodness."

The Interior Prison

T. S. Eliot's play, *The Cocktail Party,* concerns a sick society and the failure of the individual to find a way out of the supercivilised maze without calling on the nearest psychiatrist. The need of Edward and Lavinia, his wife, to work out their salvation with diligence is examined by the divine investigator (the psychiatrist) who diagnoses Edward as a man who finds himself incapable of loving, and Lavinia as a woman who finds that no man can love her. No special treatment is prescribed for their mutual failure apart from forgiveness and reconciliation. The best of a bad job, according to the psychiatrist, is all any of us can achieve. Spiritual fulfillment requires the mutual forgiveness of failure toward one another.

In *Corruption in the Palace of Justice,* Ugo Betti contemplates the possibilities of the discovery of corruption in high places, and the miscarriage of justice which could be worse than the corruption. Ludvi-Pol, a man of great power and evil repute, commits suicide in the law chambers, and the scandal of his death causes consternation among the judges, since nearly all have been involved in corruption to suit Ludvi-Pol's intents. The guilty party is known to one man when, mortally sick, takes the guilt upon himself, and leaves the guilty member to seek his own salvation in the knowledge of his rival's gesture, and in the suicide of a young girl caused through the case. The perversion of justice and of human institutions is a major area of human failure which Betti presents with artistic efficacy.

The failure of human efficiency to resolve man's fundamental existential problems is the subject of Dino Buzzatti's play, *Un Caso Clinico,* which is an astringent satire on an ultra modern hospital. Patients who are not really ill are accommodated on the top floor of a skyscraper building, and according to the gravity of the case, they descend downwards until those on the ground floor have already ceased to live. We follow the terrifying sequences of events which threaten Giovanni Corte, a formidable, tyrannical business executive who unintentionally finds himself a patient in the hospital, where he had merely gone for a consultation; as his spirit becomes more depressed, he is moved downwards from floor to floor although everyone in the hospital reassures him that there is a very good reason, and that he is behaving in his protests "like a big baby." In the end, his descent is complete, to the ground floor. With no hope, there is no alternative but to die. In this play Buzzatti has brilliantly portrayed not merely the case of an ordinary individual caught in the machinery of hospital efficiency, but the image of an ageing and dying man who fails to understand and to accept his condition.

Luigi Pirandello's *Enrico IV* offers the tragic version of a soul who relinquished the real world twenty years previously when he became mad. On regaining his sanity, he finds that he can no longer return to take up his life where he left off. He is condemned to his solitude, his lunacy, his masquerade, his despair. It is one realization of how life filters away while one breathes, and suggests that in madness alone can one find shelter. The failure to establish authentic interpersonal relationships condemns Enrico IV to the terrible anguish of loneliness. When all mutual relations are freighted with deceit and misunderstanding, the substitute world of illusion exerts a fatal attraction. Unauthenticity not only withholds oneself from others, but also expresses what is not oneself. This imposes falsehood on others; it communicate its own self-deception and falsifies its human relationships.

The stage is populated by countless others who experience, in one form or another, the anguish of failure and the pain of rejection. The dark night of the soul is the spiritual context of the orphaned, the lost, the marginal men for whom the bottom has dropped out of their lives. Others experience a different kind of failure, following upon the disintegration of meanings, of expectations and of achievements. Still others are swollen with meaningless satisfactions and dulled by petty immediacies, apparently unaware of that moral splendour that is part of the gift of life. Ultimately one's own myth will find expression, and in some way or other this expression will contain an implicit response to the universal experience of failure. It is an experience that the sinless Christ fully shared because he was fully human and fully loved us.

Chapter 3

JESUS' RESPONSE TO FAILURE

The theology of hope, with its emphasis on promises and the pull of a glorious future, requires a complementary theology of failure. Inasmuch as failure, in one form or another, is the common lot of mankind, it merits theological reflection. It is a more common experience than hope, for all men must die.

The theology of failure should contribute to an appreciation of hope as a pure, supra-terrestrial gift, for there is little evidence that man should hope for anything after death. In the face of historical evils and the inevitability of death, human hopes appear to have nothing in nature or history to sustain them. In this context hoping suggests a thoroughly inexplicable malady, an absurdity, a comfortable illusion. On the other hand it leads us to wonder whether the basis for hope is beyond nature and history. If man's hoping goes beyond death, perhaps it reflects an activity of his spirit which is even now rooted in something that transcends death. Theologians speak of Christian hope as a gratuitous gift from a supra-historical source.

Christian theologies of hope and failure have their origin in Jesus. In his absolute trust that God would accomplish his purposes through him, despite the failure of his historical mission to convert Israel, Jesus is the prototype of Christian hope. Like the prophets who preceded him, Jesus failed to convert many of his countrymen to his message and ideals. As blasphemous as it might seem for Christians to declare that Jesus died a failure with his historical mission unaccomplished, this statement would not offend secular historians.

Faith goes beyond the evidence of history, though it does not necessarily contradict it. History can verify only the Jesus that failed; faith alone can bear witness to his resurrection from the dead. The resurrection event is recognized only by faith; it is not accessible to the experience of non-faith. Faith affirms that Jesus succeeded in accomplishing his Father's will; it implies that the ways of God not only differ from those of men, but also contradict them.

Jesus' historical failure in his life's mission and the frustration of his historically manifested hopes are for Christian faith the way *par excellence* through which God revealed himself in Christ and accomplished the salvation of mankind. Jesus himself had adumbrated this mystery when he stated that he who tries to save his life shall lose it, and he who loses it for his sake will save it. Jesus "lost" his own life in failure through the infamy of a public execution. In fact, if public approval is the criterion of success, his life appears to be a greater failure than that of Barabbas.

Jesus' absolute hope in God corresponds to his willingness to accept history's verdict on the failure of his life and mission. The important thing was to be the kind of person his Father wanted him to be, even if this entailed the apparent failure of his mission. The historical failure of Jesus is a vitally important theological datum which renders Christian faith in the resurrection all the more remarkable and implies its trans-temporal character as gift. Only faith can sustain that a man who died as a failure in the eyes of the world was a "success" before God.

The Cross as a Sign of Failure

The cross is a powerful and fundamental Christian symbol of what has been achieved through the historical failure suffered by Jesus. When we say that Jesus bore his cross for the salvation of mankind, we mean that he endured genuine, radical, humiliating failure for the salvation of mankind. The resurrection "success story" of faith expresses God's verdict on Jesus' acceptance of his historical failure to accomplish his mission through the conversion of Israel. The failure is implied in Luke's account of the movement of the disciples from Jerusalem, the Holy City, to Rome. They, too, shared Jesus' failure to convert Israel. The concept of the New Israel implies a regrettable rejection by the Old Israel.

The theology of failure does not encourage fatalism, passivity, indifference to the world; rather it affirms that the man who cannot freely lay down his life is one whose ideals and values are already compromised. The man who cannot accept the possibility of complete, radical, personal failure in the carrying out of his Christian mission is not sharing that absolute poverty of spirit which characterized the freedom of Jesus to accept the divinely appointed means for his mission. In the mysterious logic of the divine Logos, there seems to be an inexorable link between the willing and courageous acceptance of complete failure in one's historical life-story, and the successful accomplishment of the divine will, which is recognized only by faith after the completion of that life-story.

The historical success of the Christian movement did not occur within Jesus' historical lifetime. It was not a part of his experience. The historical experience of Jesus was one of deep personal failure. He died a failure. The success of the Christian movement was based on the overwhelming faith-experience and interpretation of the results of that historical failure.

The theology of failure, based on the rediscovery of Christ's historical failure (the cross) and trust in a divine solution (the resurrection), has a resonance with today's revolutionary ferment throughout the world, with the longing for a new society based on social justice and peace. Such a theology must help to dispel that human dread of failure, that "prudence" which seeks peace at any price and which has become a synonym for complicity in injustice, indifference to human misery, the selfish defence of privilege, and spiritual inertia. Such a theology must remind us that there is no authentic Christianity without the willingness to risk failure and that to attempt to insulate ourselves from the possibility of failure is a betrayal of the Christian spirit, so that our attitude toward failure measures the degree of our self-transcendence in Christ.

The theology of failure counteracts the tendency to minimise the humanity and the historical condition of Jesus. Doubts about Jesus' humanity have been subtle and persistent. Docetism is the heresy which held that Jesus only seemed to be human. In its extreme forms, the incarnation was a great optical illusion or a vast pantomime. In its more subtle forms, Christians whose belief is otherwise orthodox hesitate to attribute to Jesus those aspects of the human which in more refined societies are thought to be gross or unseemly. Jesus, it is felt, could not have engaged himself in the human condition to a depth which a cultivated person would find beneath his dignity. That the historical Jesus died a failure and that his death was that of a publicly shamed and disgraced scoundrel are elements of history which the neo-Docetists shy away from.

Jesus himself emphasised his common humanity with the title "Son of Man." As for his dignity, he predicted that he must suffer (*Mt* 9:10-13; *Mk* 2:13-17; *Lk* 5:27-32). Public humiliation and execution were the historical verdict of failure on Jesus and his mission; this was the verdict which occupied the last moments on his historical consciousness before death. Paradoxically, he knew that the acceptance of failure and death was his Father's will; he had not failed to accomplish the will of his Father.

Because Jesus could not see within his historical lifetime the positive results of his acceptance of failure, his acceptance of failure and death is an act of pure faith and trust in his Father's wisdom.[1] His act recalls Abraham's faith when, despite God's promise of many children, he was willing to sacrifice his only son in response to God's will. In both cases, human reason was called to yield itself to a higher reason that was apparently incomprehensible in requiring the sacrificing of the very means for the accomplishment of the divine mission. As Jesus died, abandoned by his disciples (except John), he saw no evidence of his future community.

44

This anxiety, linked to the fear of failure, appears in Jesus' agony in the garden of Gethsemane. Like all men, Jesus instinctively hoped to avoid the possibility of failure: he did not want to die. However, through the acceptance of the inevitability of his failure as an essential part of the divine plan, Jesus attained an inner peace. His overwhelming realization of his Father's love enabled him to transcend his human fear of failure and death. Through his awareness and experience of this love, Jesus revealed that the achievement of genuine human freedom in incompatible with anxiety and crippling fears regarding the prospect of failure. The measure of our freedom in attaining self-transcendence is an index of our participation in the Spirit of Christ.

Failure and Decision-Making

Man is a decision-making animal. The inability to make responsible decisions is self-destructive. Fear of decision-making implies a rejection of the intrinsic dynamism of the human condition. Man is dehumanised to the extent to which fear of failure precludes his decision-making.

Failure appears as an inevitable part of human living in death, the failure of the human organism to sustain itself. Our attitude toward death is implicity an attitude toward failure. The fear of death may be so great that we condemn ourselves to failure on other levels of our existence that are rich with promise. Freedom of spirit means possibility, and to stand on the edge of possibility is rather like standing on the edge of a precipice. The fear of death or failure may be so great that it may preclude that human development which is attained only in responsible decision-making with regard to the possibilities for such a development. There is no human growth without decisions, and there are no decisions which do not in some way incur the risk of failure.

Through his historical decisions, including that of accepting the failure of his mission, Jesus wrought the salvation of mankind. He found the acceptance of his failure hard and agonising; intellectuals, according to St. Paul, regarded it as mere foolishness. Like man in all things except sin, Jesus experienced the heartbreak of failure as profoundly as any man before or other him. He was not obliged to accept it; there was no call on him other than that of his Father's love. Only those who love much might understand how Jesus could accept failure and how he could accept death for others. In this respect love transcends human finitude and historical disaster, adumbrating its trans-temporal source in that God whom St. John called Love and described as taking the initiative in loving us first. Love is the momentum of the salvation process which both transcends and redeems failure. It transcends, because nothing can stop it; it redeems, because for those who love God everything is a grace, a new occasion for loving him.

Judas was Jesus' failure among his disciples. Judas had all the ability, the grace, the call, the daily companionship of Jesus whose friendship he enjoyed. Although Judas knew Jesus better than we do, he failed to understand him, to share his Spirit. Ironically, Judas could not accept Jesus' failure, his poverty, his humiliation, his suffering; Judas wanted a successful, respectable, well-to-do Jesus. Judas wanted independence and he got it. The Pharisees were reasonable men whom he could understand, and they did not offer him an extravagant reward. Judas had become disenchanted with a Jesus who appeared inevitably doomed to failure. Jesus had said at the Last Supper, "I no longer call you servants but friends," and the first time he made good his promise to call the apostles friends was to Judas in the garden when he was betrayed by a kiss.

Jesus' final moments with his disciples were marked by a terrible isolation, by his profound feeling of not reaching them. There was a chasm between them; both were groping to make contact. Jesus' washing of their feet was the symbol of the entire passion: it was the work of a slave, recalling the servant of Yahweh in Isaiah. This symbolic act was the charter of the future Church. A fraternal love that transcended historical failure was Jesus' legacy, hope and desire for his members.

Jesus' symbolic act revealed that it is fraternal love, rather than historical success or failure, that counts before God. With the reception of the Spirit of Jesus at Pentecost, the disciples came to understand and experience that love, revealed and communicated through the power of the cross, which is the true meaning of Jesus' historical failure.

The mystery of Jesus' historical failure is that of the cross, and this comes out clearly in the Gospel narrative. The viciousness of men and the love of God combine to work the passion and death of Jesus. There is the treachery of a close friend, the abandonment by the apostles, and all the suffering without the counter-balancing of his Father's comforting presence; yet Jesus submits to the disgrace and opprobrium of historical failure in a way that, through the gift of his Spirit, reveals to mankind that its historical failure is not absolute, ultimate, or meaningless. Jesus' acceptance of failure and death is a sharing in the universal human condition which, through the gift of his Spirit of love at Pentecost, is revealed as a hopeful condition because love rather than failure is the ultimate possibility for all mankind. The power of Jesus' love is revealed in the mystery of the cross; it is his power to accept and transcend failure and the evils of the human condition on behalf of his friends. Jesus submits to failure in response to his Father's love and to the needs of his human family. Submission to failure is an act of love revealing and communicating itself to those for whom the condition of failure had been unbearable and ultimate; it is a new exodus act which creates and reveals the way of liberation from the condition of failure and its apparent finality.

Only he who loves much has the freedom and vitality of spirit to accept failure on behalf of his friends. The paralyzing fear of failure has no place among those who enjoy the freedom of the children of God. The gift of the Holy Spirit is the gift of that love which banishes fear.

Through the mystery of the cross, Jesus has created a new perspective which frees us from the domination of the world as the ultimate source of human happiness. This new perspective is that of love which sees all things as grace (*Rm* 8:28), enabling us to accept the limitations of the human condition good-naturedly with the broader vision of a love which even now transcends them. The mystery of the cross reveals that there is no self-transcendence without suffering and that the freedom, love and decision of Jesus can and must be shared in the attainment of that self-transcendence through which men become the sons of God. Through the gift of the Spirit of love the Christian is called to lay down his life daily in order to live in the free and unselfish spirit of Christ. Paradoxically, the mystery of the cross reveals that the key to authentic human freedom is a question of self-transcendence in an unselfish, responsible love of God and neighbour. Through the mystery of the cross man accepts God's call to the higher authenticity that overcomes evil with good.

The Time after Death

The impact of Jesus upon world history was felt after his death. The overwhelming impact of the risen Christ upon the course of world history is the basis for the Christian theology of death; it suggests that, like the risen Christ, those who die in communion with him wield their greatest personal influence in the arena of world history only after their death. They do not go off to another world after death; rather, they retain their radically personal relationship to the ground of being that underlies the created universe in which their historical lives had evolved and culminated. Jesus achieved after and through his death what he had failed to achieve in his historical existence before it. His historical mission was achieved when he transcended in death the historical conditions of human limitations and finitude.

The theology of failure averts to the continuity of human existence before and after death in terms of its prototype in Christ. It assumes, on the basis of faith in the risen Christ and his impact on the historical process, that our personal influence on the course of other historical lives does not cease with death; on the contrary, there is more reason to believe that it increases as dramatically as that of the risen Christ himself. Furthermore, it affirms that Jesus' acceptance of radical, historical failure was an indispensable condition for our personal salvation; it manifested, in the hindsight of the post-resurrection faith, the absolute freedom of the Son of God, unhampered by historical failure, and his power to transform mankind after having undergone the experience of death. Readiness to accept personal failure is an indispensable condition for that freedom of the spirit in God and Christ; a complete receptivity and openness to God are impossible without it.

The Christian belief in the communion of the saints implies that the risen Christ is joined by those who die in him and that they share in the efficacy of his state upon history after death. Death, in the case of Christ and of those who die in him, seems to be a condition for unleashing their personal impact for good upon the historical order; it seems to be a pre-condition for that greater freedom to exert a beneficent influence upon the lives of others in their historical struggle for self-transcendence and in their quest for salvation. Those who have died in Christ are invoked by the Church to exert their powers of intercession on behalf of the living. Centuries after their death, saints are believed to retain an actively beneficent relationship with the human race and its historical struggles. Like the risen Christ, they may well achieve more on behalf of the human family after their deaths than before them; like the risen Christ, their lives may have been judged as failures by purely human standards.

Chapter 4

THREE FACES OF FAILURE: DEATH - SATAN - SIN

There is a phenomenology of life and a phenomenology of death at every level of man's consciousness. There are incontrovertible signs of physical death and there are incontrovertible signs of physical life. There are similar signs at the psychic, affective, intellectual and spiritual levels of our existence which are perhaps not as immediately discerned.

Man uses metaphors to describe both his life-enhancing and his life-diminishing experiences at all these levels. Through metaphor he implies an analogy which imaginatively identifies one object with another and ascribes to the first one or more of the qualities of the second, or invests the first with emotional or imaginative qualities associated with the second. The whole nature of our language is highly metaphorical. Our abstract terms are borrowed from physical objects. Natural objects and actions have passed over into abstractions because of some inherent metaphorical significance.

Many titles which are used to express the meaning of Jesus involve metaphors. The titles are generally applied to Jesus in terms of a particular effect he has had upon our lives as members of the Christian community. A particular dimension of his impact upon our lives calls for a particular title, defining Jesus in terms of what he has done to us and continues to do for us at every level of our consciousness, in his work of redeeming the whole person in body and psyche as well as spirit. Jesus defines himself in terms of the life-enhancing impact that he has had on others, an impact which creates a community. Jesus identifies himself in terms of the community where his saving presence is felt: "Go back and tell John what you have seen and heard: the blind see again, the lame walk, lepers are cleansed, and the deaf hear, the dead are raised to life, the good news is proclaimed to the poor and happy is the man who does not lose faith in me" (*Lk* 7:29). Jesus is what he does. He *is* the light to the blind, power to the lame, purity to lepers, the word to the deaf, the resurrection for the dead, the good news to the poor and the happiness of the believer.

The effect that Jesus has had on our lives presumes a former state. The titles that we attribute to Jesus, expressing the impact of his meaning upon our lives, imply a prior state of human affairs which he has reversed and continues to reverse. That prior state is one of failure at every level which the impact of Jesus unveils for what it is. To understand a person in need, we must understand who is a person fulfilled. We find the right diagnosis of illness from a consideration of health. The Christian community's experience of Jesus as its ultimate meaning, fulfilment and salvation implies its understanding of the particular experience of failure from which he has delivered it. Hence, we must consider the meaning of Satan, Death, and Sin, and their associated metaphors describing the condition of failure which Jesus reverses by communicating to us the life and love that he receives from his Father through the gift of their Holy Spirit.

Death, Satan and Sin — three dimensions of the Old Testament's understanding of ultimate human failure — are inseparably related to Jesus' work of deliverance. The death of Jesus affects the defeat of Satan (*Jn* 12:31) and the destruction of death (*Heb* 2:14), which had entered the world through sin (*Rm* 5:12).

The Bible describes ultimate human failure in mythological categories. It employs a tissue of symbolism to clothe the mystery of death, Satan, and sin. The mythological language employed is a symbolic, approximate expression of a truth which man cannot perceive sharply and completely but only glimpse vaguely, and therefore cannot adequately or accurately express. The mythological language is consciously inadequate because it is the closest man can come to the articulation of a mystery, of a truth that transcends his full comprehension. The Old Testament's mythological conceptions of death and the nether world, of Satan and his demons, of physical and moral evil, must be re-examined for a more adequate understanding of the mystery of the cross, of Jesus' work of deliverance accomplished through his confrontation with the ultimate evil underlying all human failure.

Jesus, for Christians, is God's ultimate and final response to ultimate human failure. It is a paradoxical response, because outwardly Jesus appeared to have succumbed to death, the work of Satan and sin, in his agonizing death on the cross. He had experienced the failure of his preaching to convert Israel before having to undergo the experience of death, the ultimate human failure, whether culpable or non-culpable. Nevertheless, Jesus' death is unique. It reverses the meaning of death by making it the expression of divine love rather than human guilt, by making it the expression of that eternal life which transcends human mortality, by transforming it into the beginning of a new life whose quality surpasses anything experienced in what was best before death. Jesus has changed the meaning of death, the ultimate human failure.

Death in the Old Testament

The Old Testament was the cultural and religious matrix which conditioned Jesus' understanding of his own death. It is the same matrix for the New Testament's theology of Jesus' victory over death, sin, and Satan.

For the people of the Old Testament, Death was not experienced as an abstract power or an inexplicable fate; rather, it became personified as the Enemy (*Ps* 18:4), the Archenemy (*Ps* 5:10), the Shepherd (*Ps* 49:14), the Hungry One, the Devourer (*Ps* 56:2), The King (*Jb* 18:14), Mother Earth (*Jb* 1:21), and the Swallower (*Jb* 7:9).[1] Death employed threatening messenger demons to communicate plague and pestilence (*Dt* 32:33; *Hab* 3:5). Not only does Death await his guests in his kingdom, but he also enters the cosmos to fetch them. Jeremiah describes Death as a monster who pursues his victims as a robber and a strangler, as a kidnapper and a reaper (*Jr* 9:20).

There seems to have taken place in Israel an evolution from a mythological conception of Death to the belief in the Enemy: Satan, the Devil. Death is bent on ultimately destroying the human race and the cosmos itself. Belial (the Swallower) became a proper name for personified evil, the Devil, and was identified with Death and his kingdom, Sheol (*Ps* 18:6).

Sir Death personifies the negation of life and evidently had no part in God's original plan of creation (*Gn* 2:17). Sir Death is the Enemy, the ultimate evil and the epitome of all evil. Suffering, persecution, illness, and all forms of human misery are experienced as partial but real death, and their originators are experienced as manifestations of the Enemy, Satan. Originators of evil visibly represent the Enemy and his chaotic forces. Personal enemies, for example, communicate the lethal power of the Enemy; they are allied to him and a part of him (*Pss.* 13:3-5; 18:4).[2] Those who threaten our lives and welfare are the allies of Death, the Enemy. Human enemies and the Enemy are described as preparing a pit for the innocent (*Ps* 124); they operate as lacerating lions. The figure of Death looms from behind the wicked to oppress and destroy the innocent (*Ps* 10:9-11).

Despite a sense of the overwhelming power of Death, the Old Testament expresses the belief that Death's powers are limited. The kingdom of Death, like the primordial chaos, is under God's control, even though God is not there (*Ps* 95:4). God alone is omnipotent; Death, Satan, and evil are limited by God's power.

Those who turn away from God turn away from life. They cannot be saved from the destructive forces of Death; in fact, they are described as bound by a covenant with Death (*Ws* 1:16). By turning to iniquity, they become the prey of Death. Iniquity is contrasted with justice, which is immortal, and with the right order in creation which for Death is unattainable, because Death is no part of God's creation (*Ws* 1:13-15).

54

Isaiah warns (*Is* 28:17; 8:5-8) that those who have turned away from faith, justice, and righteousness have turned to lies and falsehood and have looked for shelter in Death, an untrustworthy partner who will destroy them. Because God is viewed as the source of life, those who turn away from him have made a covenant with Death.

God's beneficial presence, for the psalmist (*Ps* 124), means life and happiness; his absence implies danger and death. If all human life and happiness derive from the living God, all human adversity and misfortune ultimately originate from Death himself. Adversity, therefore, implies either that God has turned his face from man or that man has turned away from God. In either case, adversity and death imply human guilt and failure; consequently, there is no reason why they should enter into the experience of the innocent. The universality of death implies that even the innocent must experience the effects of human failure and guilt. All men must eventually confront Death, the Enemy; the man in straitened circumstances even now confronts him. Those who bring about his misery represent the King of Terrors and in this sense are demonic powers (*Jb* 18:14; *Ps* 22:17).[3]

Death is described as the King of Terrors who effects dismay and horror through his traps and snares, disasters and destruction, ruins and mire, darkness, winds and waters (*Jb* 18:11; 27:20; 30:15). The title implies the demonic forces over which Death rules and through which he exercises his lethal impact upon mankind. Through fear and terror life is diminished among the living. The King of Terrors can prevent the living from experiencing a fully human life, from experiencing the beneficial presence of the living God, characterized by that disposition of the human spirit which is peace. The King of Terrors destroys men through fear; the God of life sustains men through peace (*Is* 32:16). Just as fear and terror imply the presence of evil, peace implies the righteousness of those who observe God's law (*Lv* 26:6; *Dt* 28:1-14). Fear and terror should not, therefore, be the state of those who observe the law and who are innocent; nevertheless, like death, they pervade the universal human condition. Where there is fear, Death, the King of Terrors, exercises his power. Of all the emotional forces that pattern individual and interpersonal behaviours, fear has the most insidious power to make men do what they ought not to do and leave undone what they ought to do. Under its influence, and trying to escape its influence, men seem fated to give the King of Terrors a yet stronger hold upon them. The King of Terrors personifies those forces which underlie man's individual and social fear-borne follies and his errors of omission and commission. So long as God is with Israel, his people have nothing to fear from their enemies (*Num* 14:9; *Dt* 1:29). Communion with the living God, therefore, is an experience which liberates men from those fears at the root of human failure. It delivers man from the "terrors of death" (*Ps* 55:4).

Even in our day, Mircea Eliade speaks of the "terror of history" in a way that suggests a twentieth-century counter-part to the King of Terrors.[4] Eliade is concerned with the evil in man's behaviour toward others. How can man endure the catastrophes and horrors of history? Justification of monstrous historical events by the simple fact that it "happened that way" will not go far toward freeing man from the terror that these events inspire. This historicist view increasingly loses prestige, according to Eliade, as the terror of history grows worse. He concludes that, without faith in God, man is defenceless against the terror of history; despair is the only alternative. It is a despair provoked by man's presence in an historical universe in which almost the whole of mankind is prey to the continual terror of history.

When the psalmist is assailed by "Death's terrors" (*Ps* 55:4), he prays in faith to God for deliverance. When he is approaching Death (*Ps* 61:4), the Enemy, he realizes that God alone can save him. The psalmist is on the verge of despair when the threatening shadows of Death are clouding his life and darkness seems about to overwhelm him (*Ps* 13:3-5). He calls to the living God to be rescued from Death, the Enemy, the Evil One.

The condition of death from which man seeks deliverance is described in many ways. It is a comatose state of sleep (*Jb* 14:12), the condition of someone lying in the grave (*Ez* 31:18). There are no possessions, wealth and pleasure (*Ps* 49:17). There is no memory in this impersonal state where men lose their individuality. All personal relationships to God and neighbour have been forgotten in the land of forgetfulness (*Ps* 88:13). There is no knowledge. There is no awareness of what takes place among the living (*Jb* 14:21). There is no joy, no delight (*Qo* 14:16). There is no return from this irrevocable condition of darkness and gloom (*Jb* 10:22). There is no end to this state of perpetual sleep (*Jr* 51:39). By subtracting all that is positive from authentic human living, from whatever good we have experienced in life, we arrive at some understanding of the condition of the dead. This state of existence is so diminished that happiness is no longer within reach.

The condition of death is understood and expressed in a mythical and symbolical way characterized by many local aspects. It is called Sheol, the beyond, the nether world. This is the place of the after-life, frequently referred to in the Psalms, Proverbs, Job, and Isaiah. It is the abode of those who have left the divinely established order of creation and have returned to the chaotic situation from which they had been taken. It is described as a hidden, secret place (*Ps* 139:15) where man has no power and finds himself bound in a kind of prison (*Jb* 3:21). It is a wide country, a broad domain, apparently devoid of demarcation (*Ps* 31:9) and therefore a gloomy place (*Pss.* 18 and 31). It is associated with "dead land," uncultivated waste fields and deserts, waterless lands scorched by the torrid summer heat, the Arch-enemy's sphere of influence (*Is* 16:8; *Hb* 3:17; *Dt* 32:32). It contrasts with the "garden of Yahweh" (*Gn* 13:10). It is described as miry depths (*Jb* 17:1), the miry bog where man's feet do not find a hold, stability, safety, or peace (*Ps* 40:3). The idea of the "rock" is its opposite. The depths of the sea imply chaos and annihilation (*Mi* 7:19). The psalmist seeks rescue from the danger of deep waters (Ps 130:1). The chaotic power of the deep sea is God's enemy (Ps 68-23); it symbolizes the sphere of influence of Death.

The dynamic aspect of Sheol is expressed by its frequent identification with the chaotic waters encompassing the earth and threatening to make the cosmos relapse into chaos. Sheol is a material reality under our feet, extending to incalculable depths and containing the chaotic force of the primeval waters whose negative effects extend to the structured world of human existence on the surface. The dark, formless world of Sheol, like that of the primordial deep, is a world where God is absent. Both worlds are characterized by everything that is imagined to be prior and subsequent to human life.

The deluge revealed that the waters of the chaotic ocean deep continually threaten the cosmos with the return of the primeval ocean. Subduing the waters, God saved his people and led them through the Sea of Reeds; he reduced the Egyptians to chaos and destruction by throwing them into this sea (Ex 15:5). Ezekiel's lament on Tyre (Ez 27:34) implies the link between the sea and the nether world of death. The roaring surf symbolizes infernal distress (Ps 93:3; Jn 2:4). Raging waters (Ps 124:4), breakers and waves (Ps 88:8) express the life-diminishing aspects of anxiety, confusion, and human desperation.

The evil connotations of the subterranean dark waters and primordial ocean carry over into the pit, waterpit, cistern and the grave. When the earth is opened for burial of the dead, the pit (grave) is an entrance to Sheol, the underworld abode of the dead. The grief-stricken author of Lamentations feels that he is already among the dead and sharing their condition when he declares that he has been flung into the pit and that the waters have gone over his head (Lm 3:53). The pit is also associated with destruction and corruption (Is 38:17), the fate of the body in the tomb. Job's sorrow is an experience of Sheol expressed as his drawing near the pit and the waters of death (Jb 33:22).[5] The filth, corruption, and decay of the grave depict the disgusting sense of dissolution that pervades the condition of the dead; they also depict the experience of death's effects as diminishing the quality of life among the living (*Jb* 9:31). There is a note of fatalism in the realization that no one can deliver himself from the power of Death (*Ps* 89:49), as well as in the realization that Sheol is inevitable, and that it is what it is because God is absent.

The dead have been reduced to a state of desolation in a nether world of ruin, destruction, and decay (*Ps* 73:18). Their dwelling among the primeval ruins (*Ez* 26:20) implies that death has ruined and destroyed them. They have been reduced to utter inactivity; there is no work, thought, knowledge, or wisdom in Sheol (*Ez* 9:10). They lie in dark, deep, dusty regions among the ruins of the non-world.

The power of death is symbolized by a fortress with gates and bars (*Is* 38:10) and chambers (*Pr* 7:27). The oppressive power of death is expressed by the image of a fortified city. The Israelite cries to God for help when he feels that he is drawing near to the fortress gates of Death (*Ps* 107:18).

The oppressive character of death is that of a nether world prison without light or freedom of movement (*Jr* 38:6). The psalmist declares: "You did not imprison me in the land of the Enemy" (*Ps* 31:9). Closely related to the image of death's power in terms of a prison is that of death as a house (*Is* 14:18). The grave is a "home" inasmuch as a family grave accommodates many generations. It is also a meeting house where all men are eventually reunited (*Jb* 30:23). The land of the dead is a gloomy house with many chambers, comparable to a prison.

There is no communication among the dead, nor between the dead and God, because they dwell in the land of silence. Oppressive silence pervades the impersonal, non-human condition of those who experience Sheol (*Ps* 94:17; 115:17). It is the state of absolute aloneness brought on by the lethal power of the Archenemy, Death.

The dead cannot experience beauty, for they live in a world of darkness (*Jb* 15:22). Total darkness is linked with terror (*Jb* 22:25). Man must see to know and delight in his existence, for seeing and awareness are a form of responsiveness to the world of the living. Darkness was the condition of the primeval abyss. God's first creative act was to dispel darkness through the gift of light. Darkness, rooted in chaos, is an element of evil and disorder; it is among the plagues of Egypt (*Ex* 10:22); it symbolizes defeat, captivity, and oppression (*Is* 9:1). It is the evil element in which the wicked operate (*Jb* 24:16).

Death is associated with falling, with a fatal tottering or stumbling. An intolerable situation is identified with the reality of death, and the psalmist personifies death as the enemy into whose jaws he dreads falling, "lest my adversary should exult when I stumble" (*Ps* 13:5). The experience of deadly peril is an experience of death itself. Insecurity and the lack of encouragement from any quarter engender a feeling of staggering, reeling, or falling in a situation where there is no sure footing, "in the shifting sand" (*Ps* 69:3). The process of dying is linked with falling, with the land of descent and of nets (*Ps* 42:7).

Falling is also associated with the depth of Sheol, the abode of the dead, situated deep in the earth where all graves are merged. The depth of Sheol expresses the distance between the dead and the living. The inhabitants of the domain of Death are removed and alienated from God and the human community, and therefore from life.

Every kind of misery implies the presence of Sheol, the presence of the powerful Foe, a situation controlled by Death, the sway of the Evil One. It implies an experience of the conditions which pervade that nether world where Death, the Archenemy, reigns. The afflicted psalmist expresses a real but partial experience of death (*Ps* 18:5f). Afflicted by failure, misfortune, and illness, the psalmist begs God to lift him from Sheol, to heal him and restore him to life (*Ps* 30:3). In this context, to be healed is to be restored to life; however, such a life implies far more than the absence of physical death. The psalmist prays for a life worth living — a full, happy, active, free, healthy life with the possibility of being and of becoming oneself in harmony with God and neighbour: "I am afflicted above measure; give me life, O Lord, according to thy Word" (*Ps* 119:107). Death, on the other hand, is experienced in the lack of a full life and in the lack of opportunities for development, for becoming fully human through the enjoyment of communion with God and neighbour.

The requisites for an authentically human life are implied by the imagery for the condition of death, because each image indicates the deprivation of an authentically human need. The land of silence implies the need for communication with God and neighbour. The chaotic waters of the primordial deep imply the need for a justly structured social order. The prison implies the need for freedom. Darkness implies the need for intelligence and beauty. Enemies imply the need for friends. The miry bog implies the need for confidence, security, and reliability. The condition of sleep implies the need for awareness and creative activity. The "dead land" of the empty, desolate, desert wilderness, the country hostile to man, the lifeless land where the demons prowl and where the briars grow — such images suggest that man needs community for his salvation. He needs a creative social climate that will foster and sustain his personal development and happiness; he needs recognition, respect, and encouragement from others. All the images imply a need for a full life sustained by communion with God and neighbour; however, each image suggests different dimensions of this relationship, both individual and social.

The images and symbols of death imply the human need for a liberation from evil on many levels. Father Pedro Arrupe, general of the Jesuit Order, spells out the need for such a liberation in his monograph "Witnessing to Justice," asserting that the evils from which liberation is required recall the evils implied by the Old Testament's symbols of death:

Liberation, first of all, from the inner constraints, the inner slavery of personal sin and sinful proclivities. Liberation, next, from the ignorance, the apathy, and the fatalism, the narrow and selfish mental patterns and attitudes induced in us by our own sins and the sins of others. Liberation, finally, from the unjust economic, social, and political structures, arrangements and procedures which effectively exclude so many people from human development, and even deprive them of the means to acquire that development for themselves.[6]

The New Testament categories of life and death cannot be fully appreciated without an understanding of their Old Testament derivation. The liberating work of Jesus presupposes the Old Testament's categories of life and death. In the Gospel of St Luke, for example, Jesus appears as the liberator of the "captives" and the "oppressed" who are suffering from disruptive forces in life. The disruption is caused by the devil's activity, including demon possession. Mental disorder and physical disease are seen as the devil's work. Jesus' acts of healing effect something of the "release of captives" and "the liberation of the oppressed" (*Lk* 13:10, 17). These acts proclaim God's breaking of the power of evil (*Lk* 11:20f); they bespeak a liberation to those who feel in the grip of evil and of the lethal forces of Sheol.

Jesus frees man from the oppression of sin and guilt with his assurance of God's forgiveness. He is himself free of such oppression and therefore able to communicate his own freedom. He liberates the outcasts of society by communicating to them his sense of being beloved of the Father, of being wanted by God (*Lk* 5:29; 19:1-10).

Jesus emancipates man from the fear of death. His raising of the dead (*Lk* 7:11-17; 8:49-56) symbolizes the release which Jesus has achieved from the dreaded effects and power of death. That life which really counts is not destroyed by death. After the resurrection it is clear that death, the Archenemy, no longer has the last word on human destiny. Death is no longer the final, ineluctable, supreme failure and disaster for mankind.

Jesus confronts Satan, the Archenemy, through whom death has entered the cosmos. Satan brings it about that Jesus is put into the hands of his enemies who threaten to reduce Jesus to nothingness and outward destruction (*Lk* 22:39-46). The primordial forces of chaos operate at the peak of their intensity to annihilate the creative work of God. But while Satan and his lethal forces of destruction outwardly have Jesus in their power, there are important ways in which they never control Jesus, and so he becomes the liberator of mankind by defeating them.[7]

First, they never succeed in overcoming Jesus' absolute trust in God. Jesus is content to entrust himself entirely to his Father, despite the taunts of rulers, soldiers, and a fellow victim. He leaves his security and his life to God. He is completely free from the control and power of the forces of evil; hence, he can liberate others.

Second, Jesus freely lays down his life for others. His God-centred life and his generous love for others are undefeated by the powers of evil and death. Jesus is not governed by expectation of return or the evil attitudes and reactions of others (*Lk* 6:27-36). His love and concern for others are absolutely free of selfish motives.

Third, the resurrection of Jesus (*Lk* 24:1-53) was an experience which convinced the disciples that death had not terminated the living relationship between Jesus and themselves. Jesus returns to be a real force in the life of the disciples and the world. His return is that of a liberator, demonstrating that the powers of evil, sin, and death are limited, and that the power of God's living and loving relationship with man is ultimate and without end.

Jesus rescues man from ultimate failure in its threefold aspects of Death, Satan, and Sin.[8] St Luke's Gospel, therefore, gives prominence to terms that in the Old Testament describe God's work of deliverance. Jesus is called "Saviour"; he achieves God's work of "salvation." Zacchaeus' change of heart is described as "salvation," indicating the kind of deliverance that Jesus brings (*Lk* 19:9). Jesus "redeems" man, denoting God's ransoming of his people from their enemies, with the stress on "deliverance" rather than on the payment of a ransom. Jesus redeems man from the Archenemy, from Death, from Sin, the ultimate evil. The result of his action is "peace," the enjoyment of harmony with God and neighbour. Jesus creates true peace (*Lk* 1:79; 2:14; 19:38) by delivering man from the grip of evil and the Evil One (Death, Satan, Sin). Jesus empowers men to "go in peace" (*Lk* 7:50; 8:48). His deliverance is a work of reassurance against evil. The deliverance which Jesus has accomplished is that work of peace, salvation, and God's reign adumbrated in the Old

Testament (*Is* 52:7). This is the "good news" which Jesus brings and partly expressed in his healing miracles (*Lk* 4:18; 9:6). It is the message of the early Church (*Ac* 5:42).

Against the background of the Old Testament's symbolism for death and the nether world, the meaning and mission of Jesus take on a deeper significance. The New Testament's names for Jesus illuminate his meaning and mission in rescuing man from the power of Death, Satan, and Sin: ultimate human failure. Dr Vincent Taylor's study, *The Names of Jesus,* discusses all the names and epithets applied to Jesus in the New Testament, some fifty-five in number.[9] They represent different aspects of God's merciful response in Jesus to ultimate human failure.

The names of Jesus ar summarised under various headings. The principal names and titles of Jesus are: Jesus, The Son of Joseph, The Son of Mary, Rabbi, Teacher, Master, The Prophet, Christ, The Christ, Jesus Christ, Christ Jesus, The Lord Jesus Christ, Our Lord Jesus Christ, Jesus Christ Our Lord, Our Saviour, The Son of David, The Son of Man, The Servant, The Lord, The Son of God, The Son, His Son, and The Only-Begotten Son. The messianic titles are: The King, He That Cometh, The Holy One, The Righteous One, The Judge, The Lion of the Tribe of Judah, The Root and Offspring of David. The Bright and Morning Star, and He That Hath the Key of David. Messianic and communal names are: The Bridegroom, The Shepherd, The Author or Pioneer, The Stone, The Head of the Body, and The True Vine. Soteriological titles are: The Saviour, The Mediator, The High Priest, The Lamb, The Paraclete, and The Expiation. Christological titles proper are: The Image of God, The Radiance of the Divine Glory, The Light of the World, The Bread of Life, The Door of the Sheep, The Resurrection and the Life, The Way and the Truth and the Life, The Firstborn, The Power and the Wisdom of God, The Last Adam, Alpha and Omega, The First and the Last, The Beginning and the End, The Beloved, The Word, and The Amen.

The titles and names concerning radiance and light counter the evil symbolized by darkness; the rock counters the miry bog; the titles concerning beginnings counter the death imagery of the end, ruin, and destruction; those concerning life counter those of death; those concerning strength counter the images of weakness, fatal tottering, and falling; The Beloved counters The Enemy; The Lamb counters The Devourer; The Mediator and The Word counter the silence associated with the condition of death and forgetfulness. Each title implies the way of the merciful Father's healing and deliverance from evil through Jesus' confrontation with the powers of ultimate failure.

The descent of Jesus into the underworld, professed in the Creed, represents the rescuing act of God. To enter into the underworld is to enter into the power of death and out of that condition from which only God can rescue, because in him are the source and origin of life. Jesus places himself in the power of death to penetrate the kingdom of death and rob it of its power. Death is no longer master in his own house, for since Jesus descended into the underworld (1 P 3:19), he has in his possession the keys of the kingdom of death (Rv 1:18). Jesus is the first man that death has not been able to detain (Ac 2:24). Death still remains the last enemy which man must finally overcome (1 Co 15:25); however, the faithful Christian lives and dies in the Lord who has overcome ultimate human failure (Rm 14:7).

"Almost twenty centuries have elapsed since the Christ-event took place, and yet no completely satisfying over-all explanation of that fact has been proposed," states Joseph Mitros, S.J.[10] The development of theological studies and the progress of sciences and philosophy have opened new vistas concerning the origin of man and his physical and moral state, and concerning the problem of evil and liberation from it. In the light of these achievements the new data must be evaluated, the old data revised, and all of them integrated before more satisfying answers can be found.

Despite the failure to provide a completely satisfying over-all explanation for the Christ-event, there has been no doubt among Christians about the real experience of the risen Christ which transformed the apostles and created the Church. The apostolic, evangelical, patristic, and contemporary theological attempts to explain the Christ-event originate in the reality of Christ's unique resurrection experience, the effects of which are shared in varying degrees by the members of his body. The various orthodox explanations of the Christ-event derive from particular dimensions of the risen Christ's impact upon human experience. For example, the new vision of reality, created by the experience of the risen Christ, is the basis for an attempt to explain the Christ-event in terms of enlightenment. Clement of Alexandria taught that the incarnate Logos illuminates the believer with his own incomparable light. Athanasius and Cyril of Alexandria wrote eloquently of Christ as the light of the world and as the giver of the Spirit of truth, transforming mankind through enlightenment. Love, joy, peace, patience, kindness, goodness, fidelity, gentleness, and self-control (*Ga* 5:22) are the qualities produced by the risen Christ's enlightenment of the human spirit.

There was no single formulation of the doctrine of the Christ-event in the patristic period. The exemplarist tradition tends to describe the impact of the risen Christ primarily in terms of moral regeneration, a redirection of the human spirit. The Western liturgical tradition tends to view it in terms of what Christ's self-sacrifice has achieved for others. The Eastern liturgies express the impact of the event as a *rescue* and a *healing*. Christ the victor has enabled us to experience a deliverance from evil, whereas Christ the illuminator explains our entry into an awareness of a life-giving reality. Man is brought from darkness to light, from the power of evil to God. The experience is explained not only as a rescue by a saviour, but also as a healing of the effects of sin through the agency of a healer. The experience of the *lex orandi,* of communion with the risen Christ in prayer, stimulates theological reflection on the Christ-event throughout the centuries. The resurrection is both the act of God on behalf of man and the transformation of man in relation to God — both realized in Christ.

For every doctrine which seeks to express the impact on human lives of the Christ-event, the elements of act and process, divine and human, once-for-allness and human fulfilment are essential. The multiple dimensions of the on-going process of human fulfilment introduced by the Christ-event find expression in both the traditional and new theologies of salvation. The saving impact of the risen Christ on human lives is interpreted according to different models of various cultures throughout the centuries. Every model that serves to explain how man may enjoy life more fully illuminates the experienced meaning of the risen Christ among his people.

Chapter 5

FAILURE DIALECTIC:
CHRIST AGAINST TEMPTATION

Temptation expresses the human proclivity to serious moral
and spiritual failure, to personal and social disintegration. Both
individuals and nations may be "tempted" to pursue self-
destructive policies; both may be "tempted" to be unreason-
able and irresponsible. Temptations appeal to the dark side of
man: potentialities for boundless self-centredness, for pride
and conceit, ruthless ambition, dishonesty and deceit, hatred
and hostility, brute or seductive abuse of others. They conceal
themselves in a variety of seemingly virtuous attitudes, of
apparently authentic values, of ostensibly respectable behaviours. Temptation may be dormant but it is never absent;
it may be thwarted but never annihilated. The Christian must
pray always lest he succumb to it. The Christian life is a
continual confronting and overcoming of the temptation
seriously to fail God and neighbour, without whom there is no
authentically human life at any level. Temptation is confronted
by striving to recognise false thoughts, beliefs, affects, desires,
images, assumptions; by trying to discern them for what they
are before God. Overcoming temptation is a dimension of
communicating Christ.

A Definition

Both K. Rahner and H. Vorgrimler define temptation as
"that which incites us to sin," and explain that to become
activated, human freedom must undergo the experience of

values, whether real or apparent.[1] To the extent that this necessary motivation to activity in human life takes the form of concupiscence, which pursues its particular good independently of man's universal moral good and can never be wholly integrated into a man's fundamental option for the good, motivation to moral evil becomes the characteristic form of temptation which occurs in the present order of things after the Fall. This temptation persists in man despite his rejection of it and consequently makes his situation obscure to him. Man cannot, therefore, boast of certainty of his salvation. At the same time, persistent temptation does not destroy man's freedom and responsibility (1 Co 10:13). With God's grace it can be overcome, if we watch and pray (Mt 26:41). It can be overcome by faith and hope (Ep 6:16), and by active asceticism.

That which incites us to sin is an element of the human condition antecedent to our free decision. It may be understood in terms of our cosmic context (the principalities and powers), or in terms of our own inner dispositions (sarx). The principalities and powers are those world forces which lie in the power of darkness (Ep 6:12). They are those forces which saturate the atmosphere of the world with values opposed to those revealed in Christ. The world that is hostile to God is everything in the world that incites to sin and embodies sin in the human environment. Although Christians cannot help being "in" the world (Jn 17:11), they cannot be "of" the world (Jn 18:36). Sarx is everything in man that resists the gift of the Holy Spirit (1 Co 5:5; Ga 5:16ff).

Attractive Illusions

In his quest for authentic values, man is tempted to believe that his entire well-being is to be found in himself alone, or in one person alone, or in one object alone. It is the temptation to transfer all his possible motivation to one created object which he must possess for his happiness. Man is tempted to self-centredness, self-interest, self-aggrandizement, self-concentration. He is tempted to refuse self-transcendence, to imagine

70

that he will find light and love in himself alone. He is tempted by illusory desires, by a fantasy life which protects him against reality, which distorts daily events, which cushions the impact of truth, and sustains him in a make-believe world of his own creation. He is tempted to a twilight of fantasy and illusion, a counterfeit life, in which he will not have to respond to values outside himself which he should respect, cultivate and foster. He is tempted to withhold himself from others by presenting a self which he is not. He is tempted to use others for his own satisfactions, to manipulate them to minister to his own desires under the guise of friendship or love. Fear and insecurity tempt him to withhold himself from whatever might illuminate his need for help; for an authentic life of the self develops only through a candid openness to the reality in oneself, in others and in the world. Temptation would ultimately alienate man from his true or real self and from the one and only universe in which he can enjoy authentic existence. If the devil is "a liar and the father of lies" (*Jn* 8:45), his programme for the "life" of the self is among his greatest deceptions.

The Meaning of the Tempter

Satan or the devil appears frequently in the Bible as the agent of temptation who even tempts Christ. He appears as the prince of this world (*Jn* 12:31), representing all the false ideals which dominate society. Satan disguises himself as an angel of light (2 *Co* 11:4), inciting opposition to God as an apparent friend of man. His temptations are associated with separation from God, mastery of the secular world (*Mt* 4:8ff), his power to manipulate human minds (*Mt* 4:3), and denial. Satan tempts man to refuse to acknowledge and to accept the truth of his own reality in particular and of reality in general. Such denial is linked to the desire for mastery of reality by the effort to destroy the truth which one finds repugnant. To have to behold the truth that has been denied is at the root of evasion and violence. Satan's temptations have the character of contractual obligation: "No man can serve two masters . . . .

71

You cannot serve God and Mammon" (*Mt* 6:19). The assumption is that every man has chosen to ally himself to the true God or to his adversary, that he has placed himself under a higher power to obtain what he believes best in life, and that he is contractually obligated to the power. Man implicitly recognizes that there is no way of independent existence which is completely safe and provided for.

The ways in which we think of Satan imply the ways in which we understand temptation. St Ignatius of Loyola's reference to Satan as "the enemy of the human race" implies, for example, the hostility of temptation to man's authentic well-being as an individual and in society. Satan's expulsion from heaven and his being "put on his own", implies the character of temptation to withdraw man from communion with God in quest of a pseudo-independent existence. Inasmuch as Satan symbolizes the absolutely separated and alienated personal existence in conflict with every other existence, there is reflected the nihilistic character of temptation which makes naught of everything except only one's own self-will. Also the separation between God and one's "own little god."

Jacques Lacarriere, in his story of the desert monks of ancient Christendom (*Men possessed by God*), implies the internal character of temptation when he writes that any desert ascetic, watching a visitor coming towards him and having a foreboding or the certain knowledge that it was the devil, sometimes discovered, when this visitor came within view, that it was none other than himself, his own double, come to meet him from the distant horizon.

Demon, adversary, phantom — these characteristics explain the devil's many functions: a beguiling, tempting creature, representing all the enticement of the world and its beauty, but also a monstrous being who frightens and attacks the monk, a repugnant, repulsive bogey of a spirit. The temptations and struggles of the Fathers of the desert alternate between those two representatives of diabolical power, Horror and Beauty.

In one case, the Tempter is presented in human and even super-human form: as a person of astounding beauty or an angel of light. Early Greek Christians depicted the devil as a handsome, charming young man or woman. They recognised that evil is so attractive and powerfully seductive that men "cede" or "consent" to its temptation. The appropriate symbol for the Tempter had to be personal and appealing; it had to be apparently good.

The art of the Middle Ages preferred to portray the Tempter as an ugly and horrifying monster. It stressed the effects rather than the cause of man's succumbing to temptation. The horrifying subhuman shape, part man, part animal, symbolized personal evil which alters and deforms the natural, corporeal and spiritual integrity of man.

Guilt, moral pain, psychoses and neuroses deprive the spirit of man of its natural equilibrium and integrity; hence, it is appropriately symbolized by a personal, deformed, quasi-bestial, or less-than-human figure. Hence, the face of the Tempter (Satan) could reveal something of beast, self, or angel. Underlying each of these possible appearances is a correlative and genuine human experience of temptation and its evils.[2]

Temptation is view as a seduction to which man is likely to yield. Jesus warns his disciples to pray that they may not come into temptation, for the reason that however willing the spirit may be, the flesh is weak (*Mt* 26:41). It is in this sense that the petition of the Lord's prayer that the Father may not lead us into temptation is to be understood (*Mt* 6:13). In the biblical thought of the Old Testament, which is implicit here, God may very well lead one into temptation, as he did Job and Abraham. The prayer asks that the Christian may be delivered from the seduction of sin, in the sense in which deliverance is assured in Revelation 3:10 and 2 Peter 2:9,[3] the apocalyptic literature in which temptation is regarded as a characteristic of the eschatological tribulations.

Idolatry

Temptation, as an incitement to sin, involves the *aversio a Deo* that is understood at the same time as a *conversio ad*

73

creaturam. It involves the basic sin of idolatry, the tendency to found life upon creatures, perhaps on oneself, to understand life and give it meaning in terms of finite creatures alone, to the exclusion of that ultimate meaning and value revealed in Jesus Christ. Temptation is the incitement to give to a creature the importance that should belong to God alone; the only possible result of this must be a terrible distortion of our existence. St Paul, speaking of the perversion of man's life through sin, climaxes his argument by pointing to idolatry as the source of the trouble: "They exchanged the truth of God for a lie and worshipped and served the creature rather than the Creator" (*Rm* 1:25).

Rather than to acknowledge and communicate the gifts of God, including the gift of oneself, man is tempted to idolise himself and his powers. He is tempted to that sin of pride which perverts human relationships. As in every temptation, it involves a misplaced commitment which expresses itself in sinful acts. It is misplaced because it ultimately enslaves man, estranging him from his authentic self, from authentically personal relations with his neighbour and God. It is the temptation to make an ultimate concern of something that is not ultimate.

The worship of the true God is a liberation from the seductive and destructive force of idolatry. The liberating life, death and resurrection of Christ express the perfect worship of the true God and empower such worship. They communicate the power to become the children of God, brothers of the Son and possessors of the Spirit of the Father and the Son. Such liberation occurs in the Christian who calls the Father *"Abba"* and makes him the vital centre of his consciousness, just as the Father was and forever is the centre of the consciousness of Jesus. In this way, the Father delivers us from evil, answering the petition of the Lord's prayer: he makes himself the centre of our loving consciousness, freeing us from the seductive and destructive influences of false gods.

Temptation is an incitement to sinfulness, to the privation of total loving, a radical dimension of lovelessness. That dimension, as described by B. Lonergan,[4] can be hidden by sustained superficiality, by evading ultimate questions, by absorption in all that the world offers to challenge our resourcefulness, to relax our bodies, to distract our minds. But escape may not be permanent and then the absence of fulfilment reveals itself in unrest, the absence of joy in the pursuit of fun, the absence of peace in disgust, a depressive disgust with oneself, or a manic, hostile, even violent disgust with mankind.

Temptation might be understood in the context of break-downs.[5] What has been built up so laboriously by the individual, the society, the culture, can be destroyed by succumbing to the temptation of illusory ideas. Can the authentic values so laboriously achieved keep outweighing carnal pleasure, wealth, power? There is the temptation to consider religion an illusory comfort for weaker souls, an opium distributed by the rich to quiet the poor, a mythical projection of man's own excellence into the sky. The temptation proceeds in stages. Initially, not all but some religion is pronounced illusory, not all but some moral precept is rejected as ineffective and useless, not all truth but some type of metaphysics is dismissed as mere talk. Hence, the elimination of a genuine part of the whole means that a previous whole has been mutilated, that some balance has been upset, that the remainder will become distorted in an effort to compensate.[6] Increasing dissolution will tempt men to increasing division, incomprehension, suspicion, distrust, hostility, hatred, violence. It will tempt men to intellectual, moral and religious scepticism; it will undermine intellectual, moral and religious self-transcendence.[7]

Temptation is an incitement to failure with regard to the basic constituents of an authentic Christian spirituality which, both as theory and praxis, will comprise *a basic vision* or *world-view*, a cherishing of the *values* embraced by that vision and a panoply of vehicles for the realization of these values. The basic sin of idolatry embodies a break-down on all three levels: a creature determines our world-view, our values and our service. It becomes the centre of our inner life's enduring underlying attitudes, assumptions and patterns; it becomes the ultimate ground of our experience, understanding and judgment.

The temptation to sin is implicitly a temptation to despair: to relinquish hope in the voluntary rejection of our consciously recognized dependence on our fellowmen and God, as well as of the corresponding duty of seeking perfection and salvation in harmony with them. The temptation may take the form of moral indifference (*accidie, acedia*) which shrinks from the effort of following Christ and which prefers one's own world-view and values to those revealed by the grace of God in Christ. Those who despair have succumbed to the temptation to live for themselves alone and arbitrarily to refuse to place their hope in Christ. They rebel against their duty of being dependent for their self-fulfilment. Ultimately every resistance to offered grace is a form of despair; it is also a form of idolatry in which man acts as his own little god, placing all his hopes in himself.

The Way of Death

Jesus sometimes used the imagery of "ways" and "gates" in depicting the journey of man towards perdition or salvation. In the Acts of the Apostles, Christians are spoken of as the followers of a "way." The ancient Christian work the *Didache* begins with these words: "There are two Ways: a Way of Life and a Way of Death, and the difference between these two Ways is great."[8]

Now just as there are many kinds of error but truth is one, so the number of possible gates or ways to destruction is infinite but the ways of life all coalesce into one: the love of God with all one's heart and soul and mind and strength and of all others in God. The ways to ultimate happiness (heaven) and to ultimate misery (hell) refer not only to the final eternal state of man's consciousness, but also to the internal state of man's consciousness here and now. The kingdom of God and the kingdom of Satan are present realities and the various ways leading to them refer respectively to certain fundamentally authentic and inauthentic modes of thinking, desiring and doing in the world. Temptation, in this context, is an incitement to inauthentic existence, to everything in man that is opposed to Christ, leading to the definitive and lasting rejection of the exigencies of the true self, the self insofar as it is understanding, rational, responsible and loving.

Temptation may be understood as an incitement to that "Way of Death" which Bernard Tyrrell describes as the "Gates of Hell" in his phenomenological analysis of inauthentic existence.[9] The temptation to *sensualism* incites man to the pursuit of pleasure and the avoidance of pain at all costs, to live by likes and dislikes, to self-indulgence and hedonism, to live dominated by desire and fear rather than by authentic meaning and value. The temptation to covetousness, *possessivism,* covers a wide range of possibilities. He is dominated by the desire to have material objects, to have a personality, to have people, to have fame. Whatever he clings to takes hold of him and dominates his consciousness like an idol. Because of a fundamental lack of trust in God, he fails to understand that man's fundamental act is to let God fulfil him, to let God's Kingdom come within him. By not allowing God's Kingdom to come within him, there will be no real having at all: "From the man who has not, even what he has will be taken away" (*Mk* 4:25). *Intellectualism* is the temptation to seek self-glorification and self-gratification through the possession of knowledge. Through the possession of knowledge, the intellectualist seeks to have power over others. He uses it as a weapon, to humiliate or demean others and to extol himself. He does not regard the truth as something that he has freely received and must freely give, but rather as "his" knowledge, separating himself from the rest of men. *Personism* is the temptation to absolutize oneself or other selves. Current trends in psychology, philosophy and religion which stress that man and not God is the centre and master of things are engaged in personolatry. Self-centred consciousness does not discern the ground of Being. Interpersonal consciousness is focused on the inter-action of the self and the other. It fails to see that background without which the foreground could not appear. The interpersonal focus tempts man to ignore the truth of what really is. The personist sees himself or other human beings as the only source of hope and love and light in the world. Personism tempts man to a way of "life" that is deluded, ignorant, darkened and diseased, and can be healed only through an acknowledgement of the transcendent God in whom all things subsist and have their being.

All the "Gates of Hell" are temptations to idolatry.[10] The sensualist makes an idol of his feelings. The possessivist turns having into an idol. The intellectualist make idols of his schemes, ideas and hypotheses. They are overcome by radical monotheism: the explicit existential acknowledgement that God alone is Absolute and that all created things are to be valued and judged and loved in the light of the Love-Intelligence in which they have their being. The radical monotheist understands that the love of neighbour is inseparably conjoined with the love of God, but adores God alone and knows that it is only through the Spirit's gift of love in his heart that he can love others with fidelity, perseverance, self-sacrifice and true commitment. The Beatitudes express the spirit of that radical monotheism taught by Jesus during his healing and enlightening mission. They express the power of God which liberates man from the spiritually fatal tendency of absolutizing himself, that seeking to save one's life which Jesus warned would ultimately lose it.

Christian ethics, according to Stanley Hauerwas, confronts a temptation which is another variant of idolatry: the understanding of himself as self-creator. Defining man as maker has not only made it impossible to account for fundamental affirmations at the heart of Christian existence; it has also made contemporary ethics unable to come to terms with the human condition in its modern dress. Contemporary ethics mirrored men's illusion of power and grandeur by its failure to emphasize the categories that could give men an appreciation for their condition as finite, limited and sinful beings; thus it has failed in its moral task. By making man's will the source of all value we have turned away from the classical insight of Christian and philosopher alike that the measure of moral and spiritual goodness ultimately lies outside our selves. The dominant image of man the maker drives God into the universe of the "wholly other," leaving the world to whatever fate man's absolute freedom determines for it; even if he is present or is the God of history, he does little more than confirm the irrepressible march of human creativity. With such a view, any life-directing attraction towards God's creative and redemptive being becomes unintelligible. Christian ethics and spirituality in such a context inevitably tend to be Pelagian; the aim of the Christian life becomes right action rather than the vision of God through a graced sharing in the mind and heart of Christ.

Waning Faith

Temptation incites us to un-faith, to a rejection of the vision of God, taken in Lonergan's sense of faith as "the eye of love," without which the world is too evil for God to be good, for a good God to exist.[11] Faith is the eye of love, the conviction that all things work together for good to those who love God (*Rm* 8:28); it recognizes the ultimate significance in human achievement. This conviction can, however, be undermined by inattention, by distractions which dominate the centre of man's consciousness: "... they are choked by the worries and riches and pleasures of life and do not reach maturity" (*Lk* 8:14). Worries, wealth and pleasure have a way of becoming ends in themselves; they may become occasions for men to look entirely to themselves rather than to God for fulfilment. Temptation derives strength from human anxiety and stupidity.

A good start and a vigorous impetus do not guarantee success in the spiritual life. Constant vigilance and care are needed, so that we do not succumb to self-deception in an atmosphere of ambiguity and obscurity which leads finally to open sin. St Ignatius Loyola remarks in his *Spiritual Exercises* that the evil spirit attracts and tempts men with things which in themselves are indifferent, that is, in no way sinful. He seeks to limit men's freedom by holding before them the illusion of greater freedom; under the appearance of good, he seeks to alienate the mind and heart from God. Consequently, an authentically Christian life must be an examined life, one in which the subject is aware of what is taking place within his thinking and desiring.

Many temptations proceed from the disorder in our natural appetites: the instinctive reaching out for what is or appears to be good for human nature in terms of food, drink, companionship, reputation, success, love, respect, affection and so on. As someone has well said, our needs are the devil's opportunities. They are all expressions of the desire we have to increase or preserve our lives, or, in the case of the sexual appetite, with the desire to preserve the life of the species. In these very needs, all of which in themselves give life, there is an ambivalence through which they can be perverted into bearers of death. Without watchfulness, self-discipline and self-control our basic needs may alienate our minds and hearts from God.

John Sheets describes the whole process of Christian living as a process of overcoming temptation in order that the total restoration in Christ might be accomplished (*Ep* 1:4-10).[12] It means the overcoming by *faith* of what corresponds only to what the eyes can see, or human reason can penetrate; the overcoming by *hope* of tendencies to impatience and discouragement with the ways of God; and the overcoming by *charity* of any compromise in our service of God.

The Temptation of Christ

Our understanding of temptation is illuminated by an educated understanding in faith of the temptation of Christ in the desert. The Gospel accounts indicate that this was one of the particularly significant events of Christ's life. These accounts aim at instructing the Christian community regarding the recurrent human situation of temptation.

The temptation of Jesus is not described as an isolated event; rather, it is linked with the description of Christ's baptism by John. These two events form two stages of one mystery. The temptation is also linked with everything that follows in Christ's public life up to its termination in death and resurrection. St Luke notes this in the final words of his description of the desert scene: "Satan left him *for a time*" (4:13).

80

Satan tempts Jesus to abandon the *kind* of messianic role he was meant to play as a suffering Messiah. He is encouraged to seek some other way of fulfilling his mission. Throughout his public life the same temptation appears in different forms. His family encourages him to work wonders at the feast day (*Jn* 7:1-4). The Scribes and Pharisees try to force his ministry into their preconceived notions about Israel's salvation (*Jn* 7:10ff). His apostles insist he should not go to Jerusalem to be put to death (*Mt* 17:21-3; *Lk* 9:21). Finally, his own humanity recoils in Gethsemane from the impending suffering and death (*Lk* 22:42ff). Throughout his temptation Christ freely decides to adhere to the way his infinitely wise Father has planned for him to fulfil his mission.

Christ responds with free decisiveness to the continuing challenges tempting him to avoid his given mission and to settle for a comfortable substitute; he was tempted to prefer a judgment based on created "wisdom" to the judgment of divine wisdom. Christ's response to Satan forms an integral part of the redemption process. On Calvary Jesus overcame evil by his obedient acceptance of death in his free choice to adhere to his Father's will. Christ's willing undergoing of death was his definitive rejection of the temptation that he find some other means for accomplishing man's salvation. His true choice sets the pattern of human response to creaturely existence in opposition to the false choice of Adam. His rejection of Satan's suggestions in the desert form part of that continuing choice which is the very heart of Christ's redemptive activity.

Satan's temptations, in the form in which he speaks to Christ, represent both false methods that Christ might employ to save men and false sources of salvation that men seek in their lives.[13]

The first and the second temptations (following the order of Matthew 4:1-11 [cf *Lk* 4:1-13]) are introduced by the expression, "If you are the Son of God . . .", which suggests that they are being presented as messianic temptations, so that implicitly the ideas of messiahship which they represent are being rejected. The first temptation, to make stone bread, suggests a "social gospel," aimed purely at the amelioration of the material conditions of life. This is set aside as inadequate because the life which Christ has come to communicate is not to be equated with the existence and well-being of the body, with vegetative and sensitive living; this would be to forget that a person lives most properly in his thought, love and freedom. The question of sustaining life tempts man to an excessive absorption in material security. To risk, or even to sacrifice one's physical health or life to safeguard and develop one's truly personal level of life is an uncommon course of action requiring both vision and courage. The fear of any threat to bodily security and prosperity tempts man to forego more truly personal values. Christ's answer, that man also lives by every word that proceeds from the mouth of God, affirms the primacy of spiritual concerns. He speaks of this primacy in the Sermon on the Mount: "Seek first the Kingdom of Heaven, and all these things shall be added unto you" (*Mt* 6:33). God's life-giving word is the creative force governing providentially the least details of our material life; but it is even much more richly life-giving as it functions in revelation to nourish the personal depths of our human living. Man is tempted to lose a proper perspective; Christ's response unveils (Satan's) false hierarchy of human values.

The *second temptation,* to leap from the pinnacle of the temple, rejects sensationalism as a way of creating belief in his messianic mission. Jesus rejects the temptation to see immediate, tangible results. This is the temptation to tempt the Lord, "to force God's hand," to put God on trial. It recalls Job's demanding that God explain himself and account for his methods. Impatience with the slow workings of God's providence tempts man to bypass the cross. Satan tells Christ to test God to see if he is faithful to his promises. Christ's reply implies that the special love which the Father has for him shall not be exercised or manifested according to the rules of merely human logic. It is the divine logic that the love of the Father for the Son and the Son for the Father shall find its expression in the less tangible, less immediate, but the ultimately all-comprehensive answer of the cross. This temptation is the encounter between the divine logic and the logic of human "reasonableness." There is the persistent temptation

82

for human "reasonableness" to give advice to God and to chide him for his methods. Man prefers his own way of accomplishing his good and often looks for the spectacular solution. After preferring our fallible judgments to divine wisdom transmitted to us in revelation, we then look to God to exercise extraordinary power to remedy our foolishness. T. W. Manson rightly says: "To thrust oneself in to peril, merely to provide God with the occasion for a miracle, is not faith but presumption."[14]

The *third temptation* is to worship Satan for the sake of world domination, and this is of course idolatry, the prizing of the creation above the Creator. Jesus rejects making worldly power his ultimate concern. His rejection of this idol runs through his mission of obedience to his Father alone. He refuses to idolize any being, his own being or humanity. In this temptation Jesus reveals the true origin of the Kingdom as the gift of the Father to the Son. The gift is related to worship, service and obedience.[15] The "father of lies" relates the gift, the service and worship to himself rather than to God. Whatever Christ does is done because it is the will of the Father; consequently, his every action is liturgical, consecrated, set aside. "For them I sanctify myself, that they also may be sanctified in truth" (*Jn* 17:19). The death of Jesus on the cross is continuous with his life and mission of loving and obedient self-giving to the Father. The Kingdom which Jesus communicates remains the gift of the Father, not of anyone else; and no one can experience its reality "unless the Father who sent me to draw him" (*Jn* 6:44). Jesus communicates the Father's gift of the Kingdom in the Father's way: "I do always the things that are pleasing to him" (*Jn* 8:29). The cross is his way: "Yes, only if I am lifted up from the earth, I will draw all men to myself" (*Jn* 12:31-33). The cross overcomes enslavements, distortions and alienations to which man falls victim through idolatry; it overcomes all opposition to the Father's love, once-and-for-all, in and through Christ. It is the divine answer to the temptation to attain ultimate happiness through self-affirmation, self-assertion and self-seeking. God the Father is the ultimate good and his Kingdom is established and communicated in his way.

The three temptations are closely related to the Christian's renouncing of the world which is at enmity with God, a renunciation made with the baptism of each Christian.[16] The Christian renounces that attitude which considers this world to be a closed system from which the Creator is excluded. This attitude is enmity with God and destroys what it loves by making the ideal of life the maximum of pleasure, or success, or dominion over others. Renunciation of the world is the renunciation of idolatry in all its forms, whether it is power, or wealth, or sex, or political ideology; it expresses the freedom and dignity of man called to share in the life of God, in his view of creatures. The hearts and minds of authentic Christians are not possessed by creatures; hence, they are free to love what is of ultimate meaning and value: the Father of Christ Jesus.

Renunciation of the world in this way is impossible without that familiarity with God which engenders an authentic sense of reliance on and submission to him; otherwise, the Christian will easily delude himself that he is serving God when he is actually serving the world. Renunciation of the world is a prerequisite for a responsiveness to the Holy Spirit. Without familiarity with God, the Christian will also be tempted to withdraw from the world as far as possible, denouncing it as evil. His worship and service of God will be ineffective unless he gives it meaning through his dedication to his work, through his thirst for justice and truth in public and private life, and by his love for his fellow men, starting with his own family. The authentic worship and service of God in Christ is not an impediment to this world's development but the condition for it; rather, those who worship themselves and prefer their own desires and ideas to the worship of God are afflicted by an existential ignorance which brings misery both to themselves and to the world.

Christians have been baptized into Christ's relationship with his Father; they participate in his lifelong overcoming of Satan's temptations and in his victory on the cross. Because the cross of Christ is the way to communion with God, the Church requires the sacramental death of each man in baptism before such communion be established in Christ, the man *par excellence* through the hypostatic union. We receive in baptism the Spirit which raised Jesus from the dead (*Rm* 8:11); we enter into the life of the Trinity, growing in that life as we die to ourselves and give ourselves entirely to God. We participate in that self-giving of the Trinity, revealed to faith through the mystery of the cross; for there is nothing that the Father has which is not wholly the Son's and the Holy Spirit's, nothing which the Son has which is not wholly the Father's and the Holy Spirit's.

Every temptation to hold back something of our lives from the Father must be overcome, if we are to ratify our death with Christ in baptism and to participate in his life with his Father and his Spirit. Putting on Christ means sharing his relationship with the Father of total self-giving and receiving. The Father will demand everything of us at the moment of our death; consequently, every moment of our lives should be a rehearsal for the moment of death, of our final, free and complete self-offering to God.[17] Every Mass rehearses the moment of our death, for we offer our lives to the Father in the death of Christ, in the spirit of his free and obedient death. His free offering denotes the absence of idolatry; his obedient offering denotes the fullness of love. We share his freedom and obedience, the saving sign of the cross and its fruits. Such freedom and obedience witness our fidelity to the gift of God received at baptism.

Temptation is extended over a period longer than the short span that we ordinarily call "the moment of temptation." All the experiences of life and all the realties that enter into those experiences are subject to judgment by two opposing value systems: the values contained in Christ's mysteries and the "works and pomps" of Satan. In our personal living there is a constant challenge to our Christian values, to which challenge (temptation) we are more or less deeply responding and so conditioning ourselves for those specific instances when these values may be more acutely brought into question.

Christ's basic attitude in answering temptation saved mankind in the climax of redemption on Calvary. Because of his total self-giving on the cross, he has received all things; the Father has glorified him. Consequently, there is nothing in this world which does not belong to him; every human activity is relevant to his Kingdom. Everything that contributes to the order, beauty and development of this world contributes to the excellence of his Kingdom and shares in its value. The true value of the authentically Christian contribution will not always be appreciated by that world which is at enmity with Christ and his Father; in fact, it will be despised, or deemed useless. However, the Christian does not look to that "world" for his norms of progress; rather, he trusts in the Father of Christ, even though that Father may seem to allow our efforts to go to ruin and ourselves to be broken as Christ was broken on the cross. Still, we believe that God manifests his power in our weakness (1 *Co* 12:9); and we believe that only when we have returned everything to him will he raise us to life again. This is the mystery of the cross whereby the Father draws us to himself by freeing us from ourselves, whereby the Father empowers us to overcome every temptation that would prevent us from becoming his sons, "So that his Son might be the eldest of many brothers" (*Rm* 8:29).

Chapter 6

CONFRONTING SOCIAL FAILURE

The Christian believes that a truly effective confrontation with failure in society is enlightened by an understanding of the mystery of iniquity and grace which penetrates the world. An authentically Christian confrontation with social ills is one that is conscious of a world lacerated by sin that is being restored by the compassion of Christ. Both sin and grace are present in the social trials and tribulations of the world and will remain until the end of time.

The social reformer who is unaware of the permanent presence of evil in the world will be tempted to promise a perfect society to his fellow men and eventually will lead them into disillusionment and bitterness. The most successful social reforms cannot remove the cross from the lives of men and society. Christian realism recognizes that even the best social structures leave men free to accept or reject his Creator, to love or to hate his neighbour. Historical experience teaches that there will be individuals and groups whose evil choices inflict suffering on others. The Gospel affirms that the way of the cross will remain the road to the resurrection. The Gospel warns of future false prophets: "Many false prophets will arise; they will deceive many, and with the increase of lawlessness, love in most men will grow cold; but the man who stands firm to the end will be saved" (*Mt* 24:11-12). There is an authentically Christian wariness about false helpers who claim to have the panacea for all human problems if only we follow their advice.

The Christian will look for certain signs to test the authenticity of social reformers and prophets. Peter L. Berger, for example, suggests a criterion for their credibility: "Only believe those whose motives are compassionate and whose programs stand the test of rational inquiry."[1]

The observance of this criterion will protect one from the ineffectiveness of compassion without reason, and from the inhumanity of reason without compassion. Berger affirms that the criminals, the fanatics, and the psychopaths can use the language of compassion in their political rhetoric.[2] But it is their voices that betray them. The thirst for domination, the intoxication with a "redeeming" system, the dark thrust of madness — these are motives that are hard to control over a period of time.

Human history will never cease to provide situations where only the promise of life and resurrection can give faith and hope and can be a source strong enough for love. In this situation the indestructible character of Christ's new life is especially manifest. Faith in his Resurrection empowers us with the vision and courage to confront the social problems created by both culpable and non-culpable human failure.

The utopian vision that characterizes the revolutionary's approach to social reform generally lacks an understanding of the relativity of societies, acceptance of the fact that in man's present state no social order is entirely satisfactory, but we are committed to work, to achieve a better order than that which now prevails. The revolutionary *illuminati* approach social change with an emotionally rousing utopianism which evades the determination of real injustices suffered. They generally refuse to deal with specific injustices; rather, they begin with the premise that a social order is corrupt, exploitative and ripe for overthrow. From that premise, anything good about the social order in question is only a cleverly disguised evil designed to deflect radicals from their revolutionary purpose. Every reform, every change short of revolution, is counter-revolutionary.

The Christian confronts the revolutionary with the question, why do you want revolution? Is it not to correct injustices that cannot be corrected without fundamental change in the political, economic and social system? If so, we must specify what these injustices are. And we must be clear about the limits of reform, even the most radical reform. It is not enough to say that the system itself is unjust, for the System is not some mythological "thing." It is the conglomerate of interacting and interlocked systems of policies and habits by which power is exercised and human behaviour is conditioned. It is nothing less than society itself.

Measured by the standard of an imagined Utopia, every "society itself" is unjust. Measured by the standards of history, in a world far short of Utopia, some societies are more just than others. Relative justice is to be judged on the basis of specific injustices and how they are handled by a society. Richard John Neuhaus argues that we exclude such a basis for judgment if we make an a priori judgment that turns injustice into justice and makes every reform a further injustice.[3]

He insists that if we are to determine the real injustices suffered in society, we must first decide what constitutes an injustice. This, in turn, requires a clear notion of what values are so important to us that we are prepared to take up arms against their systematic violation.

Reflection on the question of what is an injustice, Ladislaus Orsy, S.J. describes the *unjust person* as one who denies his neighbour what is due to him by the law of God and man; *unjust acts* as fruits of the fundamental attitude of persons who move away from the love of God and the love of neighbour; *unjust social structures* as the crystallized and articulated norms for evil action. Orsy affirms that injustice does not exist abstractly nor does it exist in acts and structures detached from persons; therefore, its contagious evil must be remedied where it has its origins: in the mind and heart of man.[4] This does not exclude changing structures and blaming unjust acts; rather, reform activities are needed on all levels and these activities will not be complete and universally effective unless they reach the source, the internal disposition of man.

The Christian awareness that man can only create a human society with real failures and limitations — not an earthly paradise — stresses cooperation, patience, tolerance. To utopian revolutionaries, of course, this is a sign of weakness. But in reality it is strength, for it recognizes that the limitations on man are not all of his own making. In the end, we shall all die. We are still the mortals with a hope for this world and for eternal life, recognising that perfection is to love God and neighbour — the neighbour with whom we actually dwell. This love is expressed and made actual when we work to humanise our world in the spirit of Christ, recognising that we are subject to the same condition of finitude and experience of failure which Christ himself endured for our salvation. Revolutionary messianic prophets, on the contrary, promise to make us like gods and to create a paradise of human self-sufficiency where there is no room for gifts from God.

While there is evil present in society through human choice and that this has a profoundly disrupting effect on the relation of man and nations, still by no means can it be implied that everything disorderly is directly the result of human moral evil. It is tempting to believe this as it does make the world less complex if we can attribute the vast disorder we see in national and international life to evil. Human finiteness, which is of itself good, is also responsible for much of the disorder in the world, as well as for much of the good. We cannot equate evil and disorder with no further qualifications. This is another way of expressing the Christian conviction that man has a real task in the world, that the existence of God does not obviate the existence of man. Man's task in the world involves the eradication of the cruder limits of finiteness by employing his knowledge to put the world in order. This is man's political and social mission and it requires labour and patience. Finite human intelligence only slowly learns to attack the real problem before him. This is the profound theological insight of James Schall, S.J.: "If a man thinks that all of the suffering and disorder in the world are due, with no further qualification, to human evil and not also to finiteness, then he will end up by calling the human condition as such evil; he will probably even rebel against being a man at all since that involve in part the recognition of finiteness as a good, not an absolute good, but a good none the less."[5]

Today social institutions are being shaken by world movements and the accumulated crises which have not yet found their solutions. With the spread of education and communications, the realisation of suffering is rapidly growing, as well as a desire to effect its cessation. International peace seems to be maintained by a balance of terror between peoples who are told, and for the most part believe, that they alone have the solutions to the problems of how seemingly ideal relations among men are to be attained.

Today there is a deep consciousness of a world divided between rich nations and poor nations, of national societies divided between rich classes and poor classes: the developed and the underdeveloped. The rapid changes characterising both international and national societies were thought to give promise of levelling the distance between the rich and the poor. It was assumed that the structures which maintained the divisions between the rich and the poor in both international and national societies possessed the inner dynamic that, with rapid change, would also correct these disparities. Industrialisation, the process producing rapid social change, failed to effect a solution to the problems it created; on the other hand, many of the solutions that it brought about occasioned further problems. The state of abundance has not resolved problems of distribution.

The Failure of Social Justice

In a world of unprecedented resources we are aware of our tragic failure to employ our freedom in allocating a generous share of our world's resources for the alleviation of worldwide poverty. Hence intelligent criticism of our national and international structures is very much in order. The sobering awareness of the common imperfections and failure of social structures makes it clear that the struggle for social justice continues to be a part of human existence in general and of Christian living in particular. By the same token we are obliged to make certain that the means of the struggle are appropriate to our imperfect state. The Christian must ask about the method of waging his struggle with the egoism and private interests of those who have power; he cannot, for example, commit himself to fomenting class hatred.

Social structures fail when they push large numbers of men to the margins of civil life. Among these we have the new poor — those excluded from social development, from the progress of culture, from responsibility. Bartolomeo Sorge, S.J., director of *Civiltà Cattolica,* has called attention to the glaring fact of the "sub-humanity" that degrades society: the men who do not count, whom one disposes of without asking their opinion, who are isolated, at times to the point of moral and physical suicide.[6]

Men need more than society; they need community. Sorge distinguishes between the two. Society goes in for plans, and excludes; community brings men together, enhancing the value of the individual personality without crushing or excluding anyone.[7] Society is cold and anonymous; it rules itself by code and under law. Community expresses the warmth of concourse, one with another, and of love in friendship. There is no substitute for that process in which men draw together in association as free and responsible agents. The Christian community must be committed to the elimination of the social failure embodied in the marginal man.

In their efforts to tackle the pressing problems of the social order, many Christians concentrate too narrowly and exclusively on the immediate task of righting the ills of the social order. As a consequence they fail to give proper emphasis to the all-important work of the religious and moral conversion of man and at times even confuse their immediate goals with the ultimate goals which belong to Christ and his Church to achieve.

The trend can readily be seen in the tendency of many advocates of social change to identify the establishment of God's kingdom with the reconstruction of a just social order. In this context freedom becomes a liberation from poverty, oppression, and discrimination rather than a liberation from sin, selfishness, and the flesh. Peace is no longer regarded as that gift which God alone can give, but is seen as an absence of violence and a state of harmony among men which man himself can effect. Justice, instead of being God's gift of holiness and righteousness, is defined in the narrow framework of human legal justice. Ultimately, when this trend is carried to the extreme, salvation itself is reduced to socio-economic well-being, and the divine messianic role of Jesus is watered down to that of a social reformer or revolutionary.

Revelation and the Social Order

Such is the trend that is at work in much of the social thinking and action today. By way of correcting this disorder, which is at root theological, we should look to what God in his revelation has said about social injustice and the responsibility his people have in this regard.

It is important, first of all, to interpret the Word of God correctly as it pertains to the task of building up a just social order in this world. While it is correct to state that both the Old Testament prophets and Jesus himself proclaim and inculcate man's serious responsibility to overcome social injustice, it is wrong to maintain that, explicitly or implicitly, such a task has been given to Israel or the Church as its primary responsibility and mission. Moreover, it is unscriptural to consider the demand for social justice in Scripture apart from its basically religious context, where as it is subsumed into the personal covenant with Yahweh in the Old Testament and into the divine economy of redemption and adoptive sonship in the New Testament.

In the Old Testament context of the religious is implicit in the prophetic injunctions on behalf of social justice. Amos, Jeremiah, and the prophets taught that fidelity to the covenant should motivate such justice and that the compassion of Yahweh for his people should be the basis of motivation for the compassion of the Israelites toward each other and toward aliens. Social reform in itself was not the purpose of the covenant nor the primary proclamation of the prophets. It was always subordinate to the primary covenant relationship between God and Israel, and as such it was both a fruit of

God's covenant love and an operative sign of its presence in the lives of his chosen people.

In any discussion of Jesus as a social reformer himself or as a model for the social apostolate, it would be helpful to remember that Jesus transformed and spiritualised the material conceptions of God's kingdom that were prevalent among his contemporaries and proclaimed a spiritual kingdom that transcends the secular order. While Jesus fed the hungry (*Lk* 9:12-17) and insisted that his disciples give drink to the thirsty (*Mt* 25:31-46), he came to give a bread that is fundamentally a bread from heaven (*Jn* 6:26-33) and to assuage a thirst that is primarily a thirst for the divine (*Jn* 4:24). Jesus comes to heal the heart and spirit of man in relation to God his Father. He also comes to heal the material and social order, inasmuch as the healing of man at the core of his being necessarily entails the healing of the whole man and his environment. This properly religious mission of the Messiah and the Church's appropriation of the mission of Jesus as its own are clearly reflected in the *Constitution on the Church in the Modern World:* "Christ, to be sure, gave his Church no proper mission in the political, economic, or social order. The purpose he set before it is a religious one" (n. 42).

A second theological reflection which can help to correct the tendency to socio-political messianism in the social apostolate concerns the intimate relationship and conjunction between the achievement of the socio-economic welfare of man and his religious and spiritual welfare. While these two areas of human life are distinct and to some degree autonomous, they are also closely interdependent. Man's social and economic well-being cannot be truly and fully accomplished in isolation from the endeavour to bring man to fulfilment on the religious and spiritual plane.

The hierarchical order and interdependence at issue here derive from the simple fact that man exists de facto not in an order of pure nature but in an order structured by man's vocation to divine sonship and his existence under sin and grace. Inasmuch as man requires divinization and supernatural healing and redemption for his well-being and fulfilment, he cannot successfully live out any major sphere of his human existence apart from God's enlightening and healing grace. As Augustine pointed out centuries ago, man can only become fully human to the extent that he becomes truly and fully divine in Christ.

In this perspective, then, one can see how the socio-economic ills of the individual and community can never be adequately healed and resolved simply at their own level or in terms of merely human aims and initiatives. They can only be fully healed in the broader context of man's supernatural growth and religious fulfilment and in terms of man's response to God's gifts of justice, peace, and love. By seeking man's welfare at the highest level the other levels and dimensions of human existence find their well-being. Jesus himself enunciated the truth of this principle when he said: "Set your hearts on his kingdom first and his righteousness, and all other things will be given to you as well" (*Mt* 6:33).

By way of summarizing in a stark fashion the central thrust of the theological reflections on the social apostolate thus far, it is useful to quote a short dialogue that once occurred regarding the role of Jesus in relation to that of other spiritual leaders and social reformers. A questioner once inquired of Bernard Lonergan what the difference was between Jesus and Gandhi or Martin Luther King. The theologian's response was brief but incisive: Jesus once commanded his followers to eat his flesh and drink his blood: Gandhi and Martin Luther King never did. The reply, of course, highlights the radical transcendence of Jesus and his mission among men. It is a point that is easily ignored today.

Overcoming Sinful Structures

While the need to affirm the religious and spiritual in the Church's social commitment is clear, of almost equal importance is the need to examine theologically the fundamental notions of sin, evil, and redemption as they enter into the elaboration of its social concern. Such a critical examination is

95

especially pertinent in our time when so many Christians fail to understand and articulate the mystery of iniquity adequately.

Many today place great emphasis on the task of overcoming the so-called "sinful structures" of human existence and society. Sinful structures are seen as those elements of established political, social, economic, or cultural systems and institutions which are morally corrupt and corrupting. They directly cause or occasion poverty, injustice, discrimination, and a loss of human dignity and freedom. As embodying sin and the consequences of sin, they must be modified, overturned, or even radically destroyed so that freedom, justice, and the opportunity for human dignity can fully emerge. For many, such is the notion of sinful structures and the challenge they present. Clearly there are divergent views both about the degree of sin embodied in existing structures as well as the suitable means for overcoming them.

What is to be said from a theological perspective on this matter of overcoming sinful structures? It is essential, first of all, to analyse and articulate more fully the notion of sinful structure. The word "sin" as applied to social institutions and economic systems clearly involves an analogous use of the term — a point that is not sufficiently recognised or explicated. Strictly speaking, sin is a spiritual reality which resides directly and immediately in the heart of man. In itself it is simply evil (the greatest of evils) and accordingly is always to be condemned and radically uprooted. Sin, however, as predicated of the structures of society, has an analogous meaning which looks to the embodiment of the consequences of sin, not to sin itself. This distinction is an important one. To the degree that it is not recognised, a paradoxical mentality exists among social reformers whereby they tend both to exaggerate the evils of the social order and to underestimate them.

We can look first to the modern tendency to exaggerate the evils of social institutions. To the extent that a social apostle tends simply to equate sin and the evils embodied in the systems and institutions of society, he will be inclined to view spch structures of society as fundamentally evil and incapable of redemption or renovation. He may even call down apocalyptic destruction on sinful human culture and its sin-ridden structures. While social reformers may not consciously and formally make such an identification, we would suggest that many are unwittingly influenced by this kind of an over-simplification. As a consequence they exaggerate the evils of the social order and tend to adopt a more militant position than is warranted.

If this unnuanced notion of sinful structures leads to an exaggeration of evil on the one hand, it leads to an underestimation of it on the other. To the extent that one looks to the reconstruction of the social order in terms of changing sinful structures rather than redeeming sinful men who continuously and inevitably create these structures, he fails to take full account of the reality of sin. More significantly, he fails to come to grips with sinful structures at their root and inevitably deals more with the symptoms of sin than with sin itself.

Although we do not deny a certain validity to the notion of sinful structures and the need to redeem them, we do think that the social apostolate is short-sighted and ineffective to the extent that it concentrates too narrowly on structures rather than persons. Ultimately, a truly just and human social order stands or falls with just or unjust men. In good measure the systems and institutions of society are as good or evil as the men who create and govern them. In this perspective, then, one must admit that sinful structures will always be with us. We make this point not to undercut or discourage the task of social reform, but to correct the false premise that social ills will be removed simply by changing from one structure to another.

As a corollary of the principle enunciated above that sinful structures are redeemed fundamentally through the redemption of sinful men, it should be noted that all phases of the Church's pastoral mission and apostolate have a direct bearing on the rebuilding of the social order. This is another point that seems to be overlooked or ignored by many today. Whenever an apostle proclaims the Gospel in power, administers the sacraments in an efficacious manner, or fruitfully teaches the

Christian mysteries, by that very fact he contributes to the task of redeeming sinful structures. At first sight this view might seem naive. One might readily object that the Church's preaching, teaching, and administration of the sacraments has had little or no effect in righting the social order. The truth remains, however, that to the degree that one grows in God's justice and love, he necessarily becomes an instrument of healing and redemption within society. No one can truly put on Christ and not be concerned and involved with the task of overcoming social ills. In the light of this truth a major reason for the Church's failure to right social evil lies in the lack of genuine zeal and holiness in the Church's pastors and ministers. Once again the problem is one of persons rather than structures.

Theological reflection on the matter of overcoming sinful structures, together with the articulation of the spiritual in the social apostolate is always in order for the on-going task of rectifying the social order. Such considerations support the basic aims, importance, and work of the social apostolate. They are offered as a means to safeguard the essentially religious character of the Church's mission and as a help to expand the narrow scope to which some in the Church today would limit the important task of rebuilding the social order.

That the good which man needs clearly transcends his purely political and human resources was recognised by Harold Hughes, the distinguished senator and former governor of Iowa. His years of political experience enabled him to understand the distinction between political and spiritual means for man's transformation and welfare as well as the more fundamental character of the latter.

When Hughes announced in 1973 that he was leaving the Senate at the expiration of his first term to accept a "compelling commitment" to work for God, he said that in his new work as a lay religious worker he would continue to direct his efforts toward many of the areas in which he had been working — alcoholism and narcotics addiction, peace, social justice, and brotherhood. He then added:

It may be asked: Why change jobs if the aims remain the

same? Why not stay where you are continuing the work for those spiritual and human value goals in our society? All I can say is this: Who can convey what is the driving force inside the individual human heart? I have an intuitive, compelling commitment to launch out in a different kind of effort that will be primarily spiritual rather than political. This new work will cut across political and religious creeds, ethnic, political and language barriers, and will, I hope, reach into other countries of the world to further better international understanding. I have long believed that government will change for the better only when people change for the better in their hearts. Rightly or wrongly, I believe that I can move people through a spiritual approach more effectively than I have been able to achieve through the political approach.

The Message of Gandhi

Gandhi's approach to social reform called for a highly developed religious life. He underscored the need for daily prayer and meditation, insisting that they not only develop the qualities which are most vital to non-violent action but that in times of crisis they reinforce and purify the will.

Gandhi believed that there must be a religious and moral preparation for effective social action. He advocated religious retreats where men could meditate for deeper insight into the existing social situation and be prepared for constructive social work. He believed in fasting at times of crisis. Without an absolute trust in God, the fearlessness necessary for engaging in social conflict would be impossible. He affirmed that a non-violent man can do nothing save by the power and grace of God. Without that power and grace he will not have the courage to die without anger, without fear, and without retaliation. Such courage comes from the belief that God dwells in the hearts of all and that there should be no fear in the presence of God.

The spiritual and moral preparation required for effective action in overcoming human failure in the social structures of a country is the work of a lifetime. Although intellectual skills are important for successful social reforms, Gandhi believed that, in the absence of spiritual and moral force, they were insufficient. A prayerful and over-riding adherence to God motivated his non-violent resistance to tyranny and oppression. Religious faith gives rise to that fearlessness which renounces violence and yet continues to resist those who have the power to kill or injure; it gives rise to that fearlessness which does not shrink from facing and dealing with the elements of failure within society, despite the threat of ridicule, hostility, and persecution.

Gandhi believed that ultimate human fulfilment is not achieved in this world. He believed that it consisted in union with God. This end can be pursued indefinitely throughout one's lifetime by seeking truth through communion with God and neighbour. God is perfectly good, a God of love; in fact, all living things have an underlying unity arising out of their relationship to God. Absolute truth is identified with God; it cannot be fully attained in this life. Gandhi, nevertheless, believed that adherence to God requires "holding firmly to the truth" (*Satyagraha*), to the extent that we can know it.

Truthfulness and loving concern for others are the two key qualities for effective social action. They are expressed by the imperatives "Tell the truth" and "Make people happy." Effective commitment to the truth about human needs requires the control of one's fears, greed, rage, and sexual passions. We must bear within ourselves the qualities that we wish to communicate to society; we cannot foster peace and brotherhood among men through deception, hatred, violence, and bad faith. Social action based on fidelity to truthfulness and concern for others will bless those who use it as well as those against whom it is used.

Through prayer and meditation the social reformer hopes to attain truthfulness and veracity so that he may avoid both self-deception and the deception of others. Adherence to the truth must not be compromised by passion, self-love, or hatred of others. Holding fast to the truth as he sees it, the reformer must also be open to recognizing the truth represented by his opponents; hence, his attitude in social conflict is that the truth will prevail. Gandhi's ideal reformer was a man of prayer, unconditionally on the side of truth and only conditionally on the side which others take to be his own, the condition being that his side should turn out to represent justice and the true good in that concrete conflict. Gandhi recognised the importance of discerning the spirit which motivates social engagement and particular decisions. One must discern whether one's motive is self-assertion or what is truly beneficial for everyone.

The spiritual and moral character of social engagement was uppermost in Gandhi's social theory for the attainment of justice and friendship among men. *Satyagraha,* his system of thought and action for countering injustice, is not a mere collection of techniques for effecting social justice without recourse to violence. It is a distinctive orientation of the human spirit possessed by an individual whether he is or is not actively resisting some injustice in his community. It is a way of life for the individual and the community. For the community, it is a way of thought and action which attempts to make creative use of social conflict so that it becomes the means of satisfying the needs of all members of the community.

Through *Satyagraha* Gandhi did not attempt to eliminate conflict, but sought to make it more creative. Through social conflicts different groups are made aware of one another's needs and aspirations; in this respect, they are an indispensable aid to social development and creative adjustment and a beneficent force within human society. Gandhi sought to transform the character of social conflict by overcoming its destructive potential and by drawing a human advantage from it. He understood conflict as a means of attaining the truth, not victory over one's opponents.

To Gandhi, opponents should not be envisioned merely as obstacles to justice, for they are capable of contributing to the best solution by calling attention to important aspects of a social problem that may be totally or partially beyond our awareness. Gandhi preferred to persuade his opponents of the justice of his immediate objectives; he attempted to induce them into a basically cooperative relationship through which the truth concerning relevant human needs was to be progressively revealed and a just settlement achieved. His attitude was flexible, because he was urging his opponents to cooperate in the attainment of a just resolution of disagreements.

The acceptance of suffering for the attainment of justice is linked to one's adherence to the truth. Gandhi believed that one is not genuinely committed to the truth unless one is willing to suffer on behalf of it. In its social context, this means a willingness to suffer for the benefit of others in the struggle to attain justice and peace for them. Social conflicts and disagreements inevitably entail suffering; nevertheless, suffering has a healing quality. Gandhi believed that no opponent was so corrupt as to lie entirely out of reach of moral appeals for social justice, especially if one's good will and willingness to suffer for the truth are sufficiently communicated. An evident readiness to suffer for an evident truth and the soul-force of non-violent resistance concur to create a situation in which everything possible is done to effect the conversion of one's adversaries in the quest for social justice. Nevertheless, Gandhi recognised the mystery of malice and ignorance, for there is never any certainty that one's opponents will respond favourably to even the strongest moral appeal. He was a consummate realist in acknowledging the mystery of failure, for the failure of intelligence, of reason, of love, of beauty, of goodness to evoke an appropriate response constitutes the human tragedy. It is reflected in the failure of Jesus, the incarnation of the wisdom and love of God, to convert Israel; it is reflected in the failure of man to call God "Abba" in response to the Spirit of love; it is reflected in the failure of man to transcend himself in response to what is true, right, and good.

Unwillingness to suffer in order to attain the social and moral welfare of others undermines one's will to resist non-violently. Hope for the conversion of one's opponents, the will to make them genuinely happy, demands the patience to await their favourable response without resorting to violence. Patience, the willingness to suffer for the happiness of others, is a criterion of our adherence to the truth and love of God;

it is an index of our communion with God and neighbour. It is through the patience of constructive work that the factors promoting violence can be countered. Patient engagement in constructive social work is a species of social therapy based on the conviction that the power of truth and love in quest of social justice will eventually overcome the forces that oppose

Gandhi's approach to healing the social ills of the human community had a profoundly religious and spiritual basis, for social concern and commitment, when motivated by a genuine compassion and desire to alleviate human suffering, reveal the love of God for the poor and the afflicted. At the same time, Gandhi was too realistic to expect even the most inspired social reform program to achieve Utopia, since perfect communion with God, and implicitly with one's neighbour, occurs only after death. On the other hand, communion with God and neighbour is possible; its realisation implies a healing process for both individual and society, rooted in prayer and a loving concern for others. Suffering, the self-giving of what Christians call the law of the cross, creatively heals the ills of society in Gandhi's system of *satyagraha*. Suffering is essential for remedying the results of both culpable and non-culpable social failure, and it can be sustained by an absolute trust in God.

Chapter 7

CONFRONTING HISTORICAL FAILURE

The law of failure is common to all civilization, according
to Oswald Spengler's *The Decline of the West*. All civilizations
pass through ages analogous to spring, summer, autumn and
winter. Empires and cultures grow old and eventually fail to
survive perils in their age which they might have surmounted
in their youth. A theme of Arnold J. Toynbee's *The Study of
History* is that the failure of civilizations always involves
something more than the mere weakness of age. They perish
because they make some fatal mistakes in meeting the complex
demands of history. Every civilization eventually fails and
perishes; every civilization eventually fails to adapt to some
new historical situation. Their final failure may derive from
the pride of power which prompts them to extend themselves
beyond the limits of their human possibilities. Reinhold
Niebuhr believes that the decline and death of civilizations is
rooted in freedom and sin, and that the fatal mistakes are
never prompted by mere ignorance.[1] The vain imagination of
sin is in them. Their death is a proof of sin in history.

Hans Meyerhoff affirms: "Man seems to have lost both the
rational key to, and the practical mastery over, his own
history, and this twofold loss has contributed to the prevailing
mood of our age that history is full of sound and fury signi-
fying nothing."[2] By eliminating the mysterious concept of
divine providence, Meyerhoff believes that the rationalists also
established the sovereignty of history as a rational domain.[3]
And by affirming that the meaning of man's history lies in this
world, not beyond, they also made this domain accessible to

human mastery; hence, man would be free to remake history in his own image. The failure of the secular faith that man could be owner and master of his own history has left, in Meyerhoff's view, a deep mark on modern culture in general.[4]

For Karl Popper, the history of power politics is nothing but the history of international crime and mass murder (including, he adds, some of the attempts to suppress them).[5] This history, he complains, is taught in schools, and some of the greatest criminals are extolled as its heroes. Such history reflects an idolatrous worship of power and success. This is, according to Popper, a false "history" which some Christians dare to see as the hand of God, whereas it represents an anti-Christian attitude,[6] for Christianity teaches that worldly success is not decisive. Christ suffered under Pontius Pilate, the man who was successful, who represented the historical power of that time; yet Pilate played a minor role, indicating when the really important event happened. The really important event was the suffering and death of Jesus, of the man who does not conquer, triumph, and enjoy success in terms of historical political power. In this respect, the worship of historical success, of the historical powers — the winners — appears as incompatible with the spirit of a religion that worships as the Saviour of mankind a man who underwent historical suffering, disgrace, and public execution.

Christians risk infidelity to the spirit of their faith if they attempt to see in history as it is recorded, in the history of power and success, the manifestation of divine preference or approbation. The early Christians believed that conscience must judge power, rather than the other way around. The spirit of the Church, like that of its founder, succeeds most in its martyrs and among its persecuted who suffer for the sake of justice and peace and in the name of its Lord. The spirit of the Church and its Lord is powerfully revealed and communicated through historical suffering and death: "The blood of martyrs is the seed of Christians." This is so true that the question arises whether the Spirit of Jesus is ever effectively communicated without suffering, whether the truth of Jesus can be adhered to without suffering and some form of rejection by society.

106

The apocalyptic writers of the Old Testament have an important message to communicate about fidelity to God during those periods of history when history most seems to defy the Spirit of its Lord. They write for the people of God when that people seems most out of step with the values of the times, when that people experiences social rejection, persecution, and a deep sense of failure, when that people painfully experiences the failure of historical developments to bring about the kingdom of God.

The basic stance of apocalyptic to history appears in connection with the conception of the unity of world history which is already to be found in Daniel's picture of the kingdoms (*Dn* 2:31ff.) and in the vision of the four beasts (*Dn* 7:2ff.). The kingdoms of the world have an origin, a character and a destiny, and what unfolds in them has been determined from the very beginning. The movement of world history represented so vividly in these symbolic pictures reveals an increase of evil. This view of history is most pessimistic in its basic assumption that a negative goal must be reached in world history, the measure of wickedness (*Dn* 8:23). World history leads to an "abyss," to a great destruction (*Enoch* 83:7). This increasing evil evidently lies in the nature of man and the kingdoms which he establishes, though it manifests itself in different ways.[7] Though apocalyptic abandons the view of a saving history to be found in the earlier prophetic interpretation of history, the apocalyptic writers were still consoled by the fact that history was completely under the control of God. Apocalyptic writers were especially interested in the divine ordering of the course of history. They recognised a strict predetermination of history and were convinced that nothing new ever happens: "The Holy One determined days for all things" (*Enoch* 92:2).[8]

The apocalyptists believed that the end was near in their own days, and they indicated the course of events that they thought would lead to the great denouement of history and the signs of the end. They did not think that this climax would arise out of history by any natural evolution; rather, they believed that it could only take place through the direct intervention of God in history. The expression of the apocalyptists' beliefs was marked by definite characteristics.

Conflict and Determinism

Conflict and struggle characterise the apocalyptic view of history. The apocalyptist, even more than the classical prophets, sees history as a battlefield where God, his angels, and his people are locked in battle with all the demonic forces of whom sinners and the pagan nations are the terrestrial tools. Two worlds result from this spiritual dualism: the present world, which is under the power of evil and doomed to the wrath of God and final catastrophe, and the world to come, in which a new universe will rejoin the heavenly realities and the just will be recompensed for their sufferings. Thus the apocalyptist resolves the problem of individual retribution on a new plane (*Dn* 12:1-3).

Determinism and periodisation characterise the apocalyptic theology of history. Historical events occur as the realisation of a divine plan inscribed on the "heavenly tablets." Although the existence of the divine judgment clearly implies that men are free, their liberty is exercised within the limits assigned to it by God. History, therefore, appears to be a rather mechanical process which guarantees the certainty of its own consummation. Apocalyptic tends to set a precise timetable for the fulfilment of God's purposes. After having affirmed God's forthcoming triumph over evil, the apocalyptist tends to make him the slave of the calendar (cf. *Dn* 8:13-14).

The apocalyptist spreads before his reader a panoramic view of history in which the course of world history is predetermined to the smallest detail, according to a fixed, meaningful plan. Certain of the goal of history, the apocalyptist infers from past history the laws according to which the course of the world will terminate. He calculates the in-breaking of the end, which is prepared for by a chain of terrestrial and cosmic catastrophes and finally resolves the conflict between God's will and present reality, between the divine goodness and

108

human wickedness. The climax of history is felt psychologically as imminent. Once history has reached the crest formed by events contemporary to the apocalyptist, divine judgment and the salvation of the just follow at once (*Dn* 7:23-27).

Because the time of the end is fixed, the present age is often conceived of as divided into determined periods. The dream-visions of Enoch divide time, from captivity to the end, into seventy periods during which Israel is given to the care of seventy shepherds (*Enoch* 89:72; 90:1, 5). Only when the seventy periods have passed can the end come. The apocalyptists generally assume that the fixed periods have nearly run out, and therefore the end is near. The kingdom does not come, even though the just deserve it, because certain fixed periods must first unfold.

The course of this age is predetermined and must run its course to completion. God himself awaits the passing of the times which he has decreed (4 *Ezra* 4:36-37). The whole of world history has been pre-recorded in heavenly books (*Enoch* 81:1-3; 103:1-2). Although the apocalyptists review long periods of time and are fond of dividing them into ages, each marked by its own spirit and character, they are less concerned with a single situation and its immediate outcome.

Apocalyptic literature is revelatory. The revelation is almost always concerned with the development of history, culminating in the end of this world and pointing to the mysteries of the future. The apocalyptic theology of history is based on revelation. Apocalyptic is the form taken by the literature of revelation in Judaism from the second century B.C. on. The revelation of apocalyptic bears on all the mysteries which are inaccessible to man's natural knowledge. God alone can make these mysteries known through his Spirit and his wisdom (*Dn* 2:19, 28) or through an angel speaking in his name.

Apocalyptic reveals mysteries of God, of the heavens where he resides, of the angels surrounding him, and of the demons opposing him. It reveals mysteries about the origins of the world and about Wisdom's government of creation. It reveals mysteries of the divine plan which governs the course of history, as well as mysteries of the destiny of the individual. In terms of these revealed mysteries, apocalyptic provides a basis for mysticism (Ascension of Isaiah 8-11; Apocalypse of Abraham 15-20), for angelology and demonology (Ethiopian Enoch 1-6; Revelation 12), and for cosmological descriptions of earth and hell (Ethiopian Enoch 17-19).

Through dreams, visions, or tours of the heavens with angelic guides, the seer learns the solution to the problem of evil and the coming of God's kingdom; he discovers the secrets of the hidden world, the reason for the suffering of the just on earth, and when and how the kingdom of God will come. Apocalyptists write as though they had received a vision involving God's cosmic kingdom and his eschatological battle to establish it. Angels acts as mediators not only of the revelation, but particularly of its explanation. Almost every earthly element acquires a symbolic value — parts of the human body, animals, colours, clothing, and numbers — for God is utilising everything for his world triumph. The literary expression of the revelation is a tissue of symbols, drawn freely from the ancient Scriptures and Oriental literature and from mythological, cosmological, and astrological traditions which often condition their meaning.

Apocalyptic pretends to be a revelation of the future up to the time in which the reader finds himself, a revelation granted to the ancient hero and kept secret until the present. The medium of the revelation is the vision, the opening of the heavens, the messages of the angels. The future is revealed in complicated symbolism which is not always interpreted in the apocalypse, but which can be explained if the contemporary history is sufficiently known. In any case, the apocalyptic theology of history treats of the course and goal of history as revealed.

The apocalyptic theology of history is characterised by pseudonymity. The apocalyptist ascribes his work to a hero of ancient times: Enoch, Noah, Abraham, the twelve patriarchs, Moses, Elijah, Daniel, Baruch, and Ezra. The conventional spokesman chosen by the apocalyptist always appears as the typical prophet whom God has entrusted with a message to communicate to men. By letting an ancient seer speak for him, the apocalyptist takes his stand in the distant past, thus gaining a vantage point from which to survey at a glance considerable periods of history (e.g., *Dn* 7-8; 10-11). The literary form is that of a vision granted centuries ago to a great personage; thus the apocalyptist actually described contemporary history.

A catalogue of catastrophes, of predicted afflictions preceding the end of the present age, characterises apocalyptic. A catalogue of stereotyped woes predicting terrestrial disasters and cosmic disturbances appears in the Assumption of Moses, the Apocalypse of Abraham, and Revelation. They are also present in such prophetic books as Joel (3:14ff.). Daniel merely states that before the end there will be a time of trouble such as there has never been before (*Dn* 12:1). This statment may have occasioned the stereotyped predictions in later apocalypses. An embryonic catalogue in Isaiah 24:18-20 may have suggested the later lists. The inter-relation between terrestrial and cosmic disturbances is in keeping with astral thinking, in which the stars have already predetermined what is to happen on earth. Jeremiah stressed the cosmic impact of Israel's sins. In the Apocalypse of Baruch (2 *Ba* 27:1ff.) there are twelve varieties of disasters which will mark the twelve periods before the dawn of the messianic age.

The esoteric character of apocalyptic was doubtless due to more than one reason. There was the danger of broadcasting its contents in some ages, and the necessity for limiting to the initiated the understanding of the meaning. Its message is represented as something to be kept from general knowledge and to be transmitted in secret. Enoch, for example, declares that his revelation is not for his own generation but for a far-off future generation (1 *Enoch* 1:2), and in the Ezra apocalypse the seer is told to write his visions in a book and put it in a secret place (2 *Esd* 12:37). The secret revelation must not be revealed before the end of time, before the epoch of the true author. With the decline of prophecy, there was the tendency to scrutinize the ancient inspired texts to find in them the answer to the difficulties of the present and mysteries of the future.

111

The apocalyptic theology of history emerged when the persecution of believers created a need for reinterpretation of history to reconcile God's lordship of history, his goodness, and the promises of the prophets with the apparent triumph of the godless wicked of the present age. This theocentric, unified view of history recognised that dualism underlying the ambiguities of man's historical situation; despite faith in God's lordship of history, it recognised the hegemony of the powers of evil and the believer's seeming helplessness in confronting it.

In the on-going historical conflict between the forces of good and evil, the apocalyptic theology of history summons believers to endurance, patience, loyalty, and hope on the basis of the divinely revealed outcome of history. The course of history will soon come to an end, and it will consist in the supreme and triumphant revelation of God himself. This theology of history looks for the end of the world to be preceded by a time of unprecedented suffering and by the domination of evil in the form of widespread disasters and all the suffering that human tyranny can bring; nevertheless, it believes that the same love which created the people of God will save this people.

The relevance of the apocalyptic theology of history appears in the generally accepted division of the Catholic theologies of history along the lines of incarnationalism and eschatology. It would be too facile to call the former optimistic and the latter pessimistic. Both accept the totality of Christian revelation without ignoring, suppressing, or rejecting any part of it. The eschatologists, however, are the heirs of the apocalyptic tradition in their emphasis on the essential transitoriness of this stage in which we live. The kingdom of God in its final perfection is not anticipated by a gradual mastery of the present age by Christ, but by the glorious return of Christ. An emphasis is placed on the law of the cross preceding the parousia. They offer theologians of history a vital sense of faith over and against history.

Romano Guardini's theology of history offers us faith

neither in man nor in history, but in God alone and in his providence. H. M. Feret finds a theology of history in John's Apocalypse. Feret believes that desire for the consummation of the kingdom of God compels his complete engagement in the world, compelling testimony within the Church to the glorious return of the Lamb. The Christian theology of history maintains a balance in affirming the sovereignty of God and the law of the cross in suffering fidelity (apocalyptic tradition) together with the humanity of Christ and active involvement in contributing to human welfare (incarnationalist tradition). The former stress the divine action in achieving salvation; the latter emphasize the importance of the human response.

Apocalyptic enjoys its greatest influence in difficult and perplexing times, especially among the poor and the oppressed; its appeal is largely due to its uncomplicated explanation for the existence of evil and its strikingly dramatic solution to the problem. It serves as a corrective to that human pride which tends to believe that man can work out his own salvation unaided and correct the ills of the world. The apocalyptic theology of history confronts the problem of evil with a view that clashes with the belief that man can create a utopia for himself through total commitment to the right social, political, or economic theory.

In the apocalypses there are profound spiritual principles which are true for every generation. The stories of Daniel, for example, are addressed to the age in which they were composed and to every age. Like the visions of the Book of Revelation, they merit attention not only to the details of their form but also to the great spiritual principles which they everywhere assume. They are spiritually true. In this respect they constitute that which is perennially relevant in the apocalyptic theology of history. An abiding truth of the apocalyptic theology of history is that every age is the last age for those living and dying in it; therefore, the end of history for them is imminent.

Apocalyptic literature proper begins with the Book of Daniel. Apocalyptic tendencies can be seen in the prophetic writings (e.g., *Jl* 2; *Is* 65; *Am.* 5:16-20; *Zc* 12-14; *Ez* 38-39). Important Jewish apocalyptic writings outside the Old

Testament are the Book of Enoch, the Book of the Secrets of Enoch, the Apocalypse of Baruch, the Fourth Book of Ezra, the Assumption of Moses, the Book of Jubilees, the Ascension of Isaiah, and the Testament of the Twelve Patriarchs. The two most important Christian apocalypses are the Apocalypse and the (non-canonical) Apocalypse of Peter.

"Apocalypse" is a Greek word meaning "revelation" or "unveiling." An apocalyptic book claims to reveal things which are normally hidden and to unveil the future. The word is applied to a particular type of Jewish writing produced between 200 B.C. and 100 A.D. Apocalyptic refers to a genre of literature and to a type of religious thought generally embodied in this genre.

Apocalyptic literature is the child of prophecy. Despite obvious differences of form between prophets and apocalyptists, both speak of their own generation because they feel divinely impelled to do so; both have a spiritual and moral message valid for their own and subsequent ages; both share a sense of the imminence of divine intervention in the affairs of this world; both recognize Yahweh as the Lord of history and are certain of history's goal; both believe that loyalty to God is all that really matters. The form and content of their message underwent modification from age to age, according to the circumstances and conditions of their day. The author of Daniel addressed his message to the suffering who were deeply loyal to the spirit of that Judaism which had learned the lessons of the prophets, whereas the great pre-exilic prophets generally addressed those whom they condemned as disloyal.

Both prophets and apocalyptists share a theology of history. Apocalyptic literature continues and develops further the prophetic interpretation of history. Whereas the prophets stress the human agency under divine providence, the apocalyptists emphasize the final and imminent act of divine deliverance. Where the prophets call for action, the apocalyptists call for patient endurance. The combined contribution to the theology of history has been highly influential. H. Wheeler Robinson affirms that in apocalyptic the underlying and presupposed unity of history becomes explicit. The tangled web of human history is resolved into a clear pattern, and all that seemed to challenge the divine purpose is now seen to be part of it, in the sense of adding to the glory of the final manifestation. The Book of Daniel, for example, presents the working out of the divine purpose in a series of historical stages, diversely pictured, yet always culminating in the final victory of God.

This clear pattern of the unity of history, according to Robinson, is a new conception found nowhere else in ancient literature:

From the prophets the conception passed to the apocalyptists, and from them, when adopted by the Christian faith, it passed into our Western civilization. Here it has been applied in many ways and to many ends in which no religious purpose or presupposition is manifest, as in economic or political theories of history. Yet the idea of such a unity was born nowhere alse than in the theocentricity of the prophetic teaching, and perhaps only there will it find full justification.[9]

Unity and Dualism of History

The apocalyptic theology of history views all history — human, cosmological and spiritual — as a unit. It makes explicit what was only implicit in the prophetic interpretation of history. For example, the revelation which is illustrated by the prophetic doctrine of the Day of Yahweh shows that God is victorious within the present world-order in the context of human history, whereas later apocalyptic literature enlarges its stage and develops a supra-mundane order.

Apocalyptic also provides the formula of resurrection for the nascent faith in something beyond death. The apocalyptists recognise that all other revelations of God's action in human affairs will appear to be of minor importance beside the final revelation. It is from the end that the meaning of the whole historical process derives, and God alone can reveal this meaning.

115

Although the cosmic aspect holds an important place in the apocalyptic theology of the end of time, it is not the determining factor. The idea of the end of the world is always secondary to that of God's coming; and God does not come because the world is going to end, but his coming brings, among other things, the end of the world. Because he is the God who creates life, the catastrophic aspect of the end of the world could never be the last word of his coming. The notion of a new creation and restoration is uppermost. There is no radical cleavage between history and the end, because the God who will reveal himself by a grandiose theophany at the end of time has already manifested himself and does not cease manifesting himself in the course of history, and all historical events are already charged with eternal significance. Loyalty to God in history will be rewarded on the last day.

The apocalyptic theology of history provides an explanation for the apparent frustration of the prophetic promises, the delay of God's kingdom, and the hegemony of evil in history despite the faithful observance of the law by the just. It has the following distinctive characteristics:

Dualism characterizes the apocalyptic theology of history. There is an *ethical dualism* which contrasts good and evil, life and death. There is a *cosmological dualism* of two opposing forces in the universe — good and evil, light and darkness — struggling with each other. God is the principle of cosmic goodness, and Satan is God's opponent and man's oppressor. The entire cosmos and its inhabitants are involved in the struggle between the powers of good and evil. God enjoys over-all control of the cosmos; Satan is his inferior in power. Both have their following among angels and men.

An *historical dualism* contrasts "this age" with "the age to come," the present time of evil, suffering, and death with a future time of righteousness, happiness, and life. It contrasts two distinct and separate ages which involve time and beyond time. The second age is not an outgrowth of the first; it is a new creation. It is God who brings about the imminent change from the first to the second age. There is little sense of a gradual development, still less of an imminent evolution toward better things, which has claimed so large a place in modern thought. The apocalyptic emphasis on the divine intervention leaves little room for human effort in man's present historical condition.

The present age is evil because it is under the power of Satan and his demons; the future age is blessed because it is under the complete domination of God. The present age of history is temporary; the future age is everlasting. The apocalyptic theology of history implies that goodness alone is eternal, for God is good, and he alone exists from eternity. Its logical correlate, evil, came into existence in the first evil being who opposed the will of God, and it continues in evil persons as long as evil persons continue to be. Nothing born of man is eternal. His empires rise and seem unshakably established, only to fall and give rise to others. He may give vent to his spirit, now in this direction and now in that, to impose a character upon his age, but it will run its course and give place to another.

The dualism of the two ages is often accompanied by a dualism of two earths. The present earth will end and be replaced by an incorrupt, newly created earth, or by the descent of the heavenly city. The disappearance of the old earth and the rise of the new one signals the beginning of God's kingdom.

Lord of History

The divine control of history underlies the apocalyptic theology of history. God is not an indifferent spectator of human affairs. The apocalyptists believe that the rise and fall of empires is not an aimless and endless futility. Over it all is God, directing all. The apocalyptists believe that God has a purpose for the world he created and that his power is equal to its achievement. They believe in the divine initiative in history for the attainment of its final goal. Such a view is fundamental to the Christian theology of history, inasmuch as the doctrine of the incarnation proclaims that God intervened in human history in the person of Jesus Christ to achieve his great and gracious purpose.

117

Whereas the prophets believed in the divine initiative and control in all history, the apocalyptists seem to reserve it for the great final act of history. The main interest of the apocalyptists is in the great final act of history; they set that act, in all its uniqueness, in sharp relief against all the history that has preceded it. They never repudiate the teaching of the prophets; consequently, they would not deny the hand of God in all history. Rather, they regard the entire course of human history merely from the human side, as the record of human greed, appression, and ruthlessness, until they come to the final outcome of history, which is understood solely and uniquely as the act of God.

If God is in all history, there are historical moments when he may be found in a special or unique degree. Thus the apocalyptists await the unique divine initiative at the end of history, when God would not use human freedom to achieve his purpose in an act which could be interpreted from the human side as man's, but when he would himself act in a way as solely his own as his act in creation had been. There would be no human side to this act, because it would not be the act of a man. Emphasis on the divine hand in all history would have obscured the uniqueness of this expected divine act. The apocalyptic theology of history is, therefore, pre-eminently eschatological. It focuses on the end of history.

The chief contribution of apocalyptic to the revelation of God in history is that it amplifies and emphasizes the conception of the kingly rule of God as the goal and consummation of history. Apocalyptic can never allow history to run out meaninglessly, nor can it envisage the final triumph of evil. All history lies under the sovereignty of God. His will shall be done on earth, however dark the present appearances. This conviction is the strength of apocalyptic. It enables the apocalyptist to sustain the faith of his persecuted co-religionists with a new perspective showing that the promises of the Holy Books continue to be worthy of belief.

The apocalyptic theology of history is a response to the problem of evil. The prophetic hope for the moral and physical transformation of the present order through the divine intervention in history has not been realised. The return of the Jews to Israel from Babylon and their fidelity to God and the law (*Ne* 8-10), which occasioned their great suffering and persecution (2 *Mc* 5-7) did not produce the kingdom of God. History appears to be so dominated by evil that it can no longer be considered as the scene of God's kingdom.

The rule of the godless, wicked nations instead of God over his righteous people confounds the devout apocalyptist: "If the world has been created for us, why do we not possess our world as an inheritance?" (4 *Ezr* 6:59). History is doomed. There is no apparent prophetic explanation for the evils of the present age. The hegemony of the godless demands a new interpretation of history, and the apocalyptic theology provides the answer.

The problem of undeserved, unexplained evil in their historical experience led the apocalyptists to extend and sharpen the prophetic contrast between man's world and God's world, between the present sinful age of history and nature and the future redeemed age of God's kingdom. Despite the divine sovereignty over the world of history and nature, both lay under the curse of sin and the burden of evil. As the Jews continued to be subjected to the domination of the godless and the wicked, they became convinced that trust in human resources for overcoming the evil of the present age was useless. Helpless in the face of evil, they drew the conclusion that the kingdom of God would be established only by a divine inbreaking into history which would overthrow the present age and banish the godless. The apocalyptic theology of history affirms that God alone can put an end to the evils of history; without his ultimate intervention, they would be interminable. Evil is evil, and of itself it can beget nothing but evil.

The progression of history from one generation to another has given the apocalyptist no evidence for believing that time, of itself, would improve things. He does not believe that the evil and suffering afflicting mankind in history would ultimately vanish through an on-going moral and spiritual evolution. On the other hand, the apocalyptist does not believe that evil could not give place to good. For the just, evil is

119

ultimately temporary in character; God will eventually sweep it away and establish good. God, rather than human resources, observance of the law, military strength, and the historical process, will eventually vanquish evil forever. He alone is the basis for man's hope that good will triumph over the evils of the present age. History in itself offers no such hope.

The apocalyptic of history is a theology of hope. It gives vivid expression to the faith of Israel in the future activity of its God. Having despaired of their own human resources, the faithful Israelites are summoned by the apocalyptists to hope in their God who needs nothing of that kind to overthrow the presumptuous and arrogant powers of this world and to introduce his divine and everlasting kingdom. Israel need no longer feel called upon to fight the battles of the Lord. In hope and patience the faithful of Israel would await the Lord's decision that the time had come. They would witness the coming upheaval of heaven and earth, and following the great judgment they would joyfully occupy the places that awaited them in the kingdom of God.

The weakness and subjection of the post-exilic community influences the shape of Israel's hope. Relatively few in number, chastened, and poverty-stricken, the Jews of the return undergo a religious renewal and are content to wait upon the Lord, leaving to him the further restoration that must still come. The second half of the Book of Daniel, the greatest of the Jewish apocalypses, pictures the conflict between the would-be Hellenizers and the guardians of religious tradition as a reflection in earthly politics of the cosmic struggle between the forces of good and evil.

There is no call to military action, even though Judas Maccabeus had taken to guerrilla warfare just at that time. The apocalyptist is a type of pacifist with no other recommendation to make than absolute fidelity to the law of God and possibly martyrdom. To remain faithful is the one duty of the faithful. It is for God in his own good time to vindicate his holy ones, vanquish their oppressors, and inaugurate his everlasting kingdom. The transcendentalism of the Book of Daniel is permeated with a joyful hope in the final act of salvation seen as so close at hand. In a short time the martyrs of Israel would be gloriously raised from the dead to share with their surviving companions in God's triumph.

The apocalyptic theology of history expresses a confidence that the best is yet to come, surpassing all that man could imagine. Because God is faithful to those who put their trust in him, he will not allow them to perish. The apocalyptists' pessimism about the world that is living without God is tempered by a lively hope that all things work together for good to those who love God. In the crucible of their affliction, they continue to hope in the living God and a glorious future. If the present world seems hopelessly evil, the apocalyptists' hope in God convinces them that this condition is not destined to last forever.

The apocalyptic hope does not look for the kingdom of God to be the product of historical forces; its source is suprahistorical. The God who will manifest himself in a mighty theophany at the end of history has already manifested himself during the course of history. History will not produce the kingdom, not even history as the instrument of the divine activity. Only the direct visitation of God can bring the divine purpose to its consummation and establish the kingdom. The Day of the Lord expresses Israel's hope for the divine breaking into history in spectacular fashion. It is the final visitation, for whatever form of existence results from it is final, bringing God's redemptive purpose to its ultimate consummation.

The apocalyptists look toward the future. Even their references to ancient and contemporary history invite the reader to look toward those future events which God reveals, or is represented as revealing, to the seer concerning the end of the present age, the punishment of the wicked, th judgment of mankind, and the ultimate triumph of God. The apocalyptic theology of history is developed in terms of what the apocalyptist hopes for the future. The apocalyptist's references to history are organised around the direction of Israel's glorious future, inviting believers to hope in the imminent judgment and the advent of unending happiness. There is a forward direction to even the most cataclysmic historical events, because God is still in control of history as the basis of Israel's hope.

Apocalyptic is not other-worldly escapism. It applies the great affirmations of prophetic faith to a dark age of persecution. The persecuting regime is only too real. It seems to triumph, but it can never have the last word. Ultimately God's purposes and God's faithful people will be vindicated. Dominion will be taken from the persecutor and given to the faithful (*Dn* 7:27).

Outcome of History

The kingdom of God is the goal of the apocalyptist's history. Sometimes it is thought of as a kingdom here on earth, sometimes as a new earth that is transformed into a fitting home for it, sometimes as in heaven. Sometimes it is thought of as a kingdom of God administered through the saints, sometimes as administered through a great personal leader who in himself embodies its spirit, by whatever title that leader may be described. Sometimes the kingdom is conceived as a temporary one, sometimes as one that will endure as long as time shall last. Sometimes there is no thought of any but those who are living at the time when it is established; sometimes there is the thought of the righteous dead who are raised to share its happiness. The Book of Revelation foresees a temporary millennium, followed by an everlasting kingdom. Despite all the variations, the great hope is that it is to be the kingdom of God.

The kingdom of God is the place where the will of God will be perfectly done; it is not a Utopia where all the clever things the apocalyptist can think of will be given reality. In the apocalyptic theology of history, the ideal world is the kingdom of God, and it is for the saints of God. No purely human plan for the reconstruction of the world will pave the way to the millennium. The only valid reconstruction will be primarily a spiritual one embodying the will of God for our world.

Whoever desires the coming of that world in which the will

of God is perfectly done must seek to further the performance of that will in himself and others. The apocalyptist desires a world of men loyal to God. He realizes that those who want such a world must seek to be themselves loyal, and to spread the spirit of loyalty: 'They that turn many to righteousness shall shine as the stars forever and ever" (*Dn* 12:3). The apocalyptists believe that they are doing the will of God by fostering loyalty, comforting and encouraging the loyal. By their loyalty the loyal are linked to the purpose of God and will be given a place by God in his kingdom.

As long as there are men in this world who reject the Spirit and will of God, Satan is in the world, striving with God for the power and dominion thereof. Evil cannot cure itself. For the apocalyptists, evil is not so much self-destroyed as destroyed by God. They await the sudden sweeping away of human iniquity and the establishment of the kingdom. They know that the struggle between good and evil will not go on forever, though history, the present age, is the stage for the struggle. The Victor will soon emerge, and that will be the end of the present age of conflict, persecution, evil, and suffering; the kingdom will be established.

History, or this present age, terminates with God's establishment of a new society which is not entirely new. It consists of those who have been historically loyal to God, and in this respect there is a continuity in the two ages between the suffering and faithful Jews and the saints of the kingdom of God. It is the same society, the same body of the loyal, enjoying a gloriously new condition of life.

Chapter 8

THE PEOPLE OF GOD CONFRONTING FAILURE

Christians believe that the final destiny of mankind is that of being conformed to the image of God in Jesus, the primal man. Jesus, the "beloved Son," is called "the image of the invisible God" (*Col* 1:13-15). Only through Jesus can man attain the likeness to God which at the first (*Gn* 1:26) was only man's in promise. God willed all men "to be conformed to the image of his Son" (*Rm* 8:29) and therefore, since there is no distinction, to the image of God. This is both an eschatological hope and, in some measure, a present reality, for "we all, with unveiled face, beholding the glory of the Lord, are being changed into his likeness from one degree of glory to another; for this comes from the Lord who is the Spirit" (2 *Co* 3:18). In order to put on the image of God, Christians must "put on love, which binds everything together in perfect harmony" (*Col* 3:14).

To see Jesus was to see the Father (*Jn* 12:45; 14:9). Men are called to communicate the likeness of God by sharing the likeness of Jesus in whom God is visible (1 *Jn* 3:2). Even in the Old Testament (e.g., *Ps* 8) the glory and the honour with which God has crowned man suggest both external beauty and inward dignity. The dignity and authority and nobility of appearance are God's gifts to man. Functionally, man imagined God in that man was to act on earth as God acts in the universe. Man represented God among creatures (*Gn* 1:26). Implicit is the notion that when man no longer images God in this way, he no longer enjoys perfect dominion over creation.

The failure of man to retain his dominion over the rest of

creation corresponds to his failure to live a life of holiness in communion with God. The effect has been a perversion and degradation of the image of God, with the resulting evil symbolised in many ways.

The Symbols of Evil

The Devil has been the classic symbol of evil for the people of God; however, he has been portrayed in various and sometimes quite different ways. Early Greek Christians depicted the Devil as a handsome, charming young man. They recognised that evil is so attractive and powerfully seductive that men "cede" or "consent" to its temptation. The appropriate symbol for evil had to be personal and appealing; it had to be apparently good. The art of the Middle Ages, however, portrayed the Devil as an ugly and horrifying monster. Its symbol of evil stressed the effects rather than the cause of evil. The medieval Devil symbolised personal evil which alters and deforms the natural, corporeal and spiritual integrity of man. Guilt, moral pain, psychoses and neuroses deprive the spirit of man of its natural equilibrium and integrity; hence, it is appropriately symbolised by a personal, deformed, quasi-bestial or less than human figure. In morality plays the Devil was presented as the deceiver of men and adversary of Christ; he could always be recognised, despite his disguise, by the limp which resulted from his fall from heaven.

Other symbolic representations of evil reveal its nature as a blemish, stain, or impurity, and, through a progressive interiorisation of evil, as a transgression, deviation, or sin, and finally, as a burden or charge weighing on conscience (culpability, guilt). The symbolisation of evil develops from the magical to the ethical. Evil, first conceived as a quality of action, comes to qualify the agent himself as evil or culpable. The symbols of stain, deviation, and burden attempt to represent the nature of evil; for Christians, they are associated with the "mystery of iniquity" which envelops mankind. Inasmuch as moral evils hinge upon human performance for their existence, they are often symbolised by the Devil, devils, and other personal beings.

The current outcropping of Satanism and the wave of interest with the occult in both film and novels (*The Devils, The Exorcist, Rosemary's Baby, The Possession of Joel Delaney, The Other, The Mefisto Waltz, The Damned*, etc.), as well as in popular cult, point to a culture which has lost its balance in a flood of symbols for evil. The Devil and kindred malignant spirits seem to be of perennial interest, although this interest is often enough not of a serious or religious nature. The fascination for the demonic, witchcraft, and the occult has happened before. Out of the rationalism of the Enlightenment sprang the witch trials; out of the heart of Scholasticism sprang alchemy. There seems to be a personal and collective unconscious which demands the creation of symbols of evil and which is served by them. Foreign devils, for example, in one form or another symbolise a threat to the integrity and existence of every society.

Foreigners, as well as people of a different race or culture, are generally regarded with suspicion. They easily become symbols of evil because they are alien; their radical difference is felt as a threat to the existence and values of the status quo. The Chinese spoke of "foreign devils," and other cultures have shared similar sentiments about foreigners.

Anglo-Saxon literature and drama are rich in "foreign devils," among which the Italians have been perhaps the most common, largely due to the religious antagonism of the Reformation. On the other hand, the Italian "devils" reveal the traditional way in which the Anglo-Saxon world thinks of Mediterranean man in particular, and of swarthy people in general. Darkness, danger and mystery are closely related concepts in the Anglo-Saxon's symbolisation of evil. (The American slogan "Black is beautiful" is meant to offset this prejudice.)

The Italian "foreign devils" had their roots in a land sufficiently within English consciousness to become an object for reflection, yet sufficiently alien so as to remain somewhat beyond comprehension. Italy was a known unknown, at once familiar and mysterious, proximate and elusive, sunlit and obscure.

The exotice and mysterious presence of Italy was strongly felt in the Elizabethan and Jacobean theatre where Italy was considered the academy of manslaughter, the sporting place of murder, the apothecary shop of all nations. English playwrights of the period comfortably assumed that the land of the pope and of Machiavelli is the home of vice and crime. John Webster, John Ford, Thomas Middleton and Cyril Tourneur, spellbound by the myth of Italian wickedness, thrilled English crowds with their Italian "foreign devils."

Machiavelli was the symbol of the Devil incarnate for most Elizabethans. His books were considered the grammar of a diabolical creed, of materialism tinged with satanism. His motive for writing *The Prince* was missed: the vision of a liberated Italy redeemed by the one thing that could unite it — the dominance of a just, firm, efficient leader. Unlike Italy, England was not a country occupied by foreigners and given over to civil conflict for which there seemed no remedy in the ordinary course of political events.

Gothic novels of the egihteenth century were filled with Italian "devils" — for example, Walpole's Manfred, Radcliffe's Schedoni and Montoni, Lewis' Coelestino and Flodoardo, Mary Shelley's Castruccio, Maturin's Schemoli and Morosino, Landor's Fra Rupert, and Moore's Zeluco. The criminal-monk type was the most common of the "foreign devils." These preternaturally malevolent monks were endowed with the qualities of a superhumanity; they inflicted grievous harm on innocent victims. They were also satanic tyrant types, sublime criminals motivated by joy in malevolence, lust, and the thirst for power. These "foreign devils" moved in the demonic underworld of caverns and dungeons, amid labyrinthine vaults and corridors, in which so much of the evil occurred. They moved in a world which has its roots in the mythic subconscious strata of our lives, the levels we now call archetypal. They symbolised those evils threatening what is English, open, clear, moral, and Protestant; they were

128

malevolent dark people menacing wholesome light people. They endangered the cherished value-system.

The recent spate of Mafia books and the success of *The Godfather* in the United States suggests that the Italian variety of "foreign devil" is still very much in fashion in the English-speaking world, and and that it is not entirely the product of Anglo-Sexon racism, religious bigotry, and imagination. When the Italian genius for organisation is perverted, there are elements for Gothic tales of terror in any epoch. Imperialism, capitalism, clericalism, fascism, and the Mafia connote large segments of human activity in which the fine Italian hand has, at one time or another, exerted a sinister influence upon millions. The Italian "foreign devils" gave the West its first prolonged experience of imperialism. They helped religion run awry in the vagaries of clericalism and over-centralisation. They promoted the usurious practices of Europe's first capitalists, bankers, and bookkeepers. Machiavellian and fascist politics, as well as Mafia crime, are among their most distinctive specialties. Hence, the English-speaking world's use of Italian "foreign devils" implies the rejection of the authentic evils which they symbolise, as well as the recognition that the excellence of human life in any society requires that it be exorcised of its devils, native and foreign, English or American and Italian.

Societies must recognise the "foreign devils" within their politics, business and social life, religion and crime before they can effectively exorcise them. Their creation of symbols for them is a first step in the process of exorcism. The evils must be named, described, and symbolised before a society can exorcise them; a vague sense of their presence is insufficient for the task. On the other hand, exorcism has its risks. The Devil is a liar. He may succeed in withholding his true name and in imputing his evil to the innocent. The exorcist must be a holy man; otherwise, he may be deceived and destroyed by the very devils he attempts to exorcise. Recent history bears witness to the catastrophic results produced by unholy men attempting to exorcise their societies of its "foreign devils."

Why should the devils afflicting society be envisioned as

foreign? Perhaps such a symbolisation of evil provides that vicarious experience of innocence which may be conducive to the attainment of a genuine personal and social wholeness. It is necessary to be able to imagine a society free of the devils that beset it before it is possible to exorcise it from those devils. Imagining them as foreign devils is one step in the process of alienating them. They are, in fact, foreign to the natural good of both the individual and society; hence, they can be envisioned as foreigners besieging them from without, as aliens who do not belong.

The symbolisation of evil in terms of foreign devils may also be a facile way of shirking responsibility for those evils threatening the integrity of the community by placing the blame for them on others. In times of national crisis, Chinese, Indian, and Jewish merchants have been regarded as the foreign devils of Asian, African, and Western nations, and, as in an exorcism, they have been expelled for the imagined good of the community. Evils besetting the Catholic community have been symbolised by both Roman and Dutch foreign devils. The Reformation might be viewed as an attempt to exorcise the Christian community of its Roman devil. Today there are those who would like to exorcise the Church of its Dutch devil; however, a heightened awareness of theological and moral complexity precludes the easy exorcisms of past times. This new awareness has also rendered the symbolisation of evil considerably more difficult. The devils have to be identified, or clearly symbolised, before the process of exorcism can get underway. Furthermore, there may be a greater reluctance to cast our devils into the outer darkness among those who may, after all, be "anonymous Christians." The line between the people of God and the Gentiles, pagans, infidels and heretics is no longer as sharply drawn as in the days when most of the Church's enemies were envisioned as those outside it. Such devils were authentically foreign. Today, evils within the Church, elements foreign to the spirit of Christ, may still qualify for symbolisation as "foreign" devils; they are "spirits" contrary to that of Christ, rather than nations or races.

Wilderness has long been a symbol of evil. Even modern authors discuss slum conditions and urban degeneracy under such titles as *The City Wilderness*[1] and *The Neon Wilderness*.[2] A study of metropolitan areas refers to "this new 'wilderness' that has grown up in Megalopolis."[3] The implication is that modern man feels as insecure and confused in an urban setting as he once felt in the forest among wild beasts and the frightening creatures of his imagination.[4]

Wilderness is the environment of the non-human and even anti-human, the place of wild beasts where the control and order which man imposes on the natural world is absent and where man is an alien presence.[5] Wilderness refers to the unruly, confused, disordered world of creatures not under the control of man. In the Old English of the eighth-century epic *Beowulf*, the term (wildeor) refers to savage and fantastic beasts inhabiting a dismal region of forests and cliffs.

Wilderness as the habitat of wild beasts implied the absence of men and a region where a person was likely to get into a disordered, confused, or "wild" condition. The semi-human wild man, for example, was the most important imaginary denizen of the wildernesses of medieval Europe. He appeared widely in the art, literature, and drama of the period. He lived in the heart of the forst, as far as possible from civilisation. He symbolised what happened to the isolated man of the wilderness, living outside the human community. He was a savage ogre who devoured children and ravished maidens.[6]

Man is "bewildered" in an alien environment where the civilisation that normally orders and controls his life is absent. Such an environment produces a state of mind in which man feels lost, stripped of guidance, perplexed, and at the mercy of alien, mysterious and malign forces. This concept has extended the meaning of the word to include large and disordered collections of things, even if man-made.

Among most early cultures paradise was man's greatest good; wilderness, as its antipode, was his greatest evil. In one

131

condition the evironment, garden-like, ministered to his every desire. ("Eden" was the Hebrew word for "delight.") In the other condition it was frequently dangerous and always beyond control. For primitive man, existence in the wilderness was precarious. Safety, happiness, and progress all seemed dependent on rising out of a wilderness situation. Human development was synonymous with man's gaining control over nature. Fire, the domestication of some wild animals, and the raising of crops were gradual steps. The reduction of the wilderness area measured man's advance toward civilisation.

The Hebrews hated and feared the wilderness as a cursed land because of its forbidding character and lack of water.[7] Men could not survive for long in such an inhospitable environment. When their God wished to threaten or punish a sinful people, he found the wilderness condition to be his most powerful weapon: "I will lay waste the mountains and hills, and dry up all their herbage" (*Dt* 8:15). Sodom and Gomorrah became parched wastes and thorny bush as a penalty for the sins of their citizens.

The identification of the arid wasteland with God's curse led to the belief that the wilderness was the environment of evil, a kind of hell populated by malign spirits. Among them were the howling dragon or *tan,* the winged female monster of the night called *Lilith,* and the familiar man-goat, *seirim.* Presiding over all was *Azazel,* the arch-devil of the wilderness. In an expiatory rite the chief priest of a community symbolically laid the sins of the group upon a goat and sent it away into the wilderness to Azazel (*Dt* 16:10). The ritual of the scapegoat reveals the Hebrew view of the wilderness.

The Old Testament treatment of the paradise theme conveys this idea of the immorality of wild country. Eden was a place without fear, the antipode of the wilderness; the creatures that lived there were peaceful and helpful. As a punishment for eating the forbidden fruit Adam and Eve were driven out of the garden into the wilderness, a "cursed" land full of "thorns and thistles." The author of Joel juxtaposes Eden and the wilderness: "The land is like the garden of Eden before them, but after them a desolate wilderness" (*Jl*

132

2:3). And Isaiah communicates the promise that God will comfort Zion and "make her wilderness like Eden, her desert like the garden of the Lord" (*Is* 51:3). The wilderness and paradise are both physical and spiritual opposites.

Wilderness, for Christians, has long been a powerful symbol applied either to the moral chaos of the unregenerate or to the godly man's conception of life on earth as a pilgrim in an alien land struggling against temptations endangering his spiritual life. Wilderness symbolises the human condition as a compound of the natural inclination to sin, the temptation of the material world, and the forces of evil themselves. In his wilderness experience of the world, the flesh, and the devil, the Christian looks to Christ and his community for deliverance. Community symbolises salvation; wilderness symbolises perdition. The Christian is supported by Christ and his community in his struggle for survival against the evils of the wilderness. He envisions his salvation in terms of the community, the kingdom, the Church of Christ, the antipode of the moral and spiritual wilderness of the lost.

Jesus formed his community to save man from the wilderness only after he had himself undergone the trials of the wilderness experience.[8] His forty days in the wilderness (desert) recalls the forty years of temptation and tribulation which Israel had undergone in the wilderness of Sinai. "Full of the Holy Spirit" (*Lk* 4:1), Jesus entered the wilderness, the natural habitat of those evil spirits which trouble men and throw them into confusion. The Hebraic folk imagination, like that of other cultures, made the wilderness the abode of demons and devils.

In his wilderness experience Jesus confronted the malign forces which beset all mankind. He experienced a genuine period of trial and suffering, a real, interior experience, more profoundly significant than the more externalised, literal interpretation in which he would actually have been taken up to the temple's pinnacle. It was an experience which, according to St Luke, was intimately linked with Jesus' death. After the temptations, the devil departed from Jesus "for a while" (*Lk* 4:13), until "the hour" of his death. Satan returned for the death of Jesus: "Satan entered into Judas" (*Lk* 22:3), and when Jesus was apprehended at Gethsemane (*Lk* 22:53), he declared: "This is your hour and the power of darkness." The insistent demands of Satan for a sign, which began in the temptations of the wilderness, continued to the end of Jesus' life with the mocking cry: "If you are King of the Jews, save yourself!" (*Lk* 23:37). The cry echoes Satan's words in the wilderness: "If you are the Son of God . . ." (*Lk* 4:3).

There is a second "echo" element in the confusion of Jesus' wilderness trial. The experience is a sequel to his baptism in which he had heard the heavenly voice saying: "You are my beloved Son." In the confusion of the wilderness, Jesus now heard another voice saying "If you are the Son of God . . ." and he had to discern whether it came from the same source. Three times Jesus concluded that the voice prompting him to action was that of Satan. He adhered to the recognition of his unique vocation in his baptismal experience and rejected all unworthy interpretations of it. He came to a realisation, for example, that he should not employ political power for the achievement of his mission. Spiritual discernment, in the face of the bewildering complexity and variety of options confronting man, is a trial from which no man is exempt.

Christ represents man's triumph over the evils symbolised by the wilderness through his submission to the basic human experience of the wilderness in his historical trial of having to discern God's will for him. Christ's ultimate accomplishment hinged upon his ability to resolve the problems of his historical mission within the given limitations of his human nature and in the face of the confusing complexity and variety of options confronting him. He did not make himself Messiah; nevertheless he had to come to the recognition of his messianic role through the normal process of human experience, understanding, reasoning, judgment, and decision. The process of coming to recognise his God-given, historical identity and mission may well have been a type of severe interior trial somewhat comparable to that of all men in quest of their historical identity, meaning, and mission.

Jesus overcame the evils of the wilderness condition in

which man feels lost and alien in a hostile world. All men are enabled to stand in the relationship of children to God precisely through the human nature assumed by Christ (*Heb* 2:14-18). Jesus is the way of the Lord through the human wilderness condition. Not only does he know the way through the wilderness, but he is the exemplar of it and manifests it in his own person. He does not merely proclaim the way; that way is inseparably connected with his person, and it is in his person that the way of God through the wilderness has appeared in the world (*Jn* 14:6). Jesus is the way to communion with God and neighbour; he is the way which re-establishes that community between God and man and among men, overcoming the wilderness condition of alienation, fear, confusion, and hostility. Because Jesus *is* the communion of God and man, union with him enables mankind to experience the same reality, the reality which is the way through the wilderness chaos to the Christian cosmos.

The wilderness symbolises the context in which Jesus and his mission have their meaning. It symbolises the human condition for which his Church, as an expression of the divine mercy, was instituted to serve as a way of liberation. Mankind's universal experience of the wilderness is the only context in which Jesus, his mission, and his Church make sense. It symbolises the experiences which Jesus knew and mastered in his own historical existence, an achievement in which all mankind participates. The personal character of the experience has been symbolised by the Devil and demons which Jesus and his disciples exorcise for the liberation of mankind.[9] Human freedom does not come without the trials of a spiritual struggle in which man must be aided by the liberating power of the way through the demon-infested wilderness of his own spirit and society (e.g., *The Asphalt Jungle, the Blackboard Jungle*).

Symbolisation of Evil: Purpose, Fruits, Dangers

Symbols suggest something else by reason of relationship, association, and convention. They are visible signs of what may be invisible as an idea or an attitude. They express an attitude, stance, orientation, or feeling. They are what they mean, and they mean what they are designated to mean. Hence, they may be transformed by the power of a new meaning. Christ, for example, has transformed the meaning of death and the cross into a symbol of salvation; he has transformed the meaning of marriage by designating it as the symbol of his union with the Church (*Ep* 5). Christian marriage is different from non-Christian marriage because its meaning is different. The sacraments are what the sacraments mean, and they mean what Christ instituted them to mean.[10] As symbols of salvation they imply counter-symbols of perdition. Our understanding of grace and evil and their presence to us in and through symbols gives the basis for the social or communal character of worship.[11]

Man is a related being who naturally expresses his relatedness through symbols. He expresses his reactions to the evils which he experiences in nature, in himself, and in society through symbols which imply his apprehension of values. His symbols of evil express his feelings of fear or aversion, and they also evoke these feelings. They have the power of expressing what man may be unable to express in a more logical and refined way; nevertheless, they complement a logical explanation by meeting a need which it cannot meet. This is the need for an affective response to the objects of his awareness.[12]

Symbols do not explain themselves; they need critical examination because they are open to multiple meanings.[13] Symbols of liberation for some are symbols of oppression for others. The explanation of the symbol goes beyond the symbol; it is necessary for the intelligent and effective use of the symbol for social action or communal worship.[14] The exorcist must know the name of (understand) the devil (the symbolised evil) before he can exorcise it; knowledge is essential for effective remedies for the evils besetting man. An erroneous understanding of the evils symbolised may lead a community to ineffectual, stupid, or even disastrous action. *Mein Kampf*, for example, provides non-economic symbols for economic ills. There is also the tendency to make the symbol the explanation for evils, as a panacea in reverse. Communism, fascism, the Vietnam War, the middle class, drugs, the Church, etc., become symbols for everything that is wrong in society.

Antithesis is an important means of persuasion, as when a policy is recommended in terms of what it is against. There is is a constant temptation of societies to achieve purgation by scapegoat, congregation by segregation. In the polemics of politics, the use of the scapegoat to establish identification in terms of an enemy shared in common enables the candidate who presents himself as spokesman for the community to prod his audience to consider local ills primarily in terms of alien figures ("foreign devils") viewed as the outstanding causes of those ills. The symboys of evil must be used wisely; otherwise, they may bring upon their users the very evils they symbolise.

Man is a symbol, the *imago Dei*.[15] His actions express and are the very meaning of his life. The good man reflects the glory of God as a visible manifestation of God's invisible nature (*Rm* 1:20); the good Christian expresses the glory of God in Christ. The same is true for the good secular society and the good society of Christians. Through evil actions, however, the symbol is perverted; it becomes, according to the measure of evil, a counter-symbol. The evil individual and society misrepresent, distort, and falsify the glory of God; the evil Christian individual and community misrepresent, distort, and falsify the glory of God in Christ. As symbols of evil, they tend to mislead man in his quest of God and his perfect image in Christ; they tend to corrupt the human understanding of God and his perfect expression in his Word. Perhaps the only evils which the New Testament reveals as provoking the anger of Christ are those misrepresentations of God and his Spirit by the official religious leaders. They had, in many respects, become counter-symbols of that God for whom Jesus was the perfect symbol. They tended to falsify the very reality which Jesus verified through his personal communication of the experience, knowledge, love and understanding of God.

The mutual love of Christians is the efficacious symbol which communicates Christ to others: "By this all men will know that you are my disciples, if you have love for another" (*Jn* 13:35). Hatred and strife among Christians is the correlative counter-symbol which misrepresents, distorts, and falsifies Christ for others. Hatred among Christians is the supreme symbol of evil because it deprives others of the authentic revelation of God's love in Christ, because it is the culpable failure to communicate the divine mercy for the fulfilment of others, and because it tends to render the meaning of God in Christ contemptible for others. The ecumenical imperative for Christians derives from their commitment to that mutual love, corresponding to that of Christ and his Father (*Jn* 15:9f), which reveals God in Christ to mankind. Ecumenical prayer services and friendly collaboration among the many Christian denominations enable Christians to become effective symbols of mutual love rather than symbols of evil.

The eucharistic *agape* and *koinonia* of the Church is the sign and the reality of Christ's salvation, that is to say, of his incarnation, death and resurrection. It is the sign that Christ is now at work in the hearts of men through the energy of his spirit, and that he is healing the fragmentation of human society deriving from sin. The Church is the community of grace, a new humanity endowed with new potentials. Although this regeneration of human life is completed in Christ, in the rest of humanity it is only inaugurated. Through the Church, the risen Christ communicates God's love for us and overcomes the separation and alienation which men experience from themselves, from their fellows, from society and from God. The power of Christ's love enables reconciliation among men which is based on a relationship of openness, response, and obedience to the overmastering reality of The Father.

Koinonia, the spiritual oneness of fraternal solidarity in Christ, reveals the transcendent goal of human life. *Koinonia* is the outward expression of that interior state of faith, hope, and love prevailing within the Church. Through this powerful expression of its interior life, the Church enlightens man to see the direction which he must follow to love God and to love his neighbour. It is this light which man needs to be himself and to rise to the dignity of a child of God. Through this power the Church brings something of the strength of

138

God to weak man. Through the gifts of the sacraments the Church has the capacity to heal the mind and heart of man. In fact, the Church's capacity to contribute to human society goes well beyond healing; for the Church reveals to man the new way of love and gives him more than human strength to fulfil the great commandment. On the other hand, the Church is aware of its limitations, recognising that it has never received a gift that would assure that out of some divine resources it would have the best knowledge for planning for economic justice or for making wise laws for social welfare. Although the Church promotes the necessary studies and responsible action, it cannot judge infallibly what is the best concrete course of action in economic, legal, and social matters when it comes to technical details. Nevertheless, despite the risk of non-culpable failure in these details, it is impelled by the transcendent source of its life to seek justice for those who suffer injustice, for those who are denied their due at any level by the actions, attitudes, or omissions of their fellow men.

The Church has a healing ministry which embraces the whole man (and society) in all departments of his being and life. Its responsibility for the health and healing of man, in the fullest sense, continues until the redemption of the whole man is complete (e.g. *Mt* 10:5-15). To be responsible for the wholeness of the individual and the community is to communicate the true meaning of the Father's love.

The Church heals the heart of man through its sacraments, the healing signs of the Church. Jesus Christ himself is understood as the Sacrament because he is "the image of the unseen God" (*Col* 1:15) and the dynamic efficacious sign of the Father's saving love for men. In Jesus Christ "lives the fullness of divinity" (*Col* 2:9), and through his saving work he has reconciled us to the Father.

The Church is itself a sacrament. In fact, the term first used to define the Church in the Constitution *Lumen Gentium* (p. 1) is sacrament. The word elucidates the Church's dynamic character in overcoming alienation, separation, hatreds and other elements of breakdown in the human community: "Since the Church is, in Christ, a kind of sacrament or sign of intimate union with God, and of the unity of the whole human race . . . she intends to set forth more precisely to all her faithful and to the entire world the nature and universal mission of the Church."

Through its fraternal charity the Church is the sign and the sacrament of God for all men. The Church is the sacrament of Christ, "the image of the unseen God," whose work she continues visibly here on earth: "Established by Christ as the fellowship of life, charity and truth, the people of God is also used by him as an instrument for the redemption of all, and is sent forth into the whole world as the light of the world and the salt of the earth" (*Lumen Gentium*, 9). The first sign of the credibility of the Church as the coming of the kingdom, the universal sign, is fraternal communion, whose source is interior union in Christ. When this love succeeds in creating a stable community between men from all parts of the earth, despite their difference of race, culture or social condition, it gives witness to that primal love at work in them to unite them.

The Church as sacrament is a universal sign of a universal love for all men: for all those who believe that the perfect unity of all mankind in love is the end for which man yearns in his inmost heart as the final fulfilment of the human community, the Church manifests herself as the anticipation, the sacrament of this unity of the human race: "this messianic people, although it does not actually include all men, and frequently has the appearance of a 'poor little flock,' is nonetheless a lasting and sure seed of unity, hope and salvation for the whole human race" (*Lumen Gentium*, 9). The Church is this sacrament of the unity which is to come by her communion with Christ and through him with God.

The Church is a communion and the pattern of communion: and we fulfil ourselves as persons only in loving the brethren in Christ. This is evidence of the truth of the paschal message: "We for our part have crossed over from death to life; this we know, because we love our brothers" (1 *Jn* 3:14). What is expressed in the liturgy carries over into the rest of life for the service of others: "They are wide of the mark who think that because we have here no abiding city but seek the city that is to come, they can neglect their duty on this earth; they forget that faith increases the obligation to fulfil those duties in accordance with their vocation. The Christian who neglects his temporal duties neglects his duties to his neighbour, neglects God and risks his eternal salvation (*Gaudium et Spes,* 43).

The goodness of a person is recognised inasmuch as that person is moved by the love of God and neighbour. So too, the goodness of Christ is communicated inasmuch as his community is moved by the love of his Holy Spirit and neighbour. It is through this movement that the final destiny of mankind, of being conformed to the image of God in Jesus, is achieved. It is through this movement that we are being transformed into his likeness and the Kingdom of God is established: for the Kingdom is where Christ is King, ruling the hearts and minds of those who are moved by his love of the Father and neighbour.

Chapter 9

THE REMEMBERING THAT TRANSCENDS FAILURE

The psalmist believed that the dead inhabit the land of forgetfulness (*Ps* 88:13) where they have lost their memory. God no longer works wonders for the dead (*Ps* 88:11). The dead are no longer capable of remembering God's wonderful works because their relationship to the living God has been severed. Sadness reigns in the world of the dead (*Dt* 34:8). Qoholeth describes the dead as those who have forgotten everything and who have been entirely forgotten (*Si* 9:5).

Because of their inability to remember God, the dead fail to share in the praise of God which characterises Israel's worship (*Ps* 88:11; *Is* 38:18). The psalmist assumes that only where there is death is there no praise of God; where there is life, there is praise. Death is characterised as the state of those who can no longer remember and therefore no longer praise God. There is no real life where there is no praising of God, and there is no praise where there is no remembering.

Through the death of Jesus, God has overcome the consequences of death, for now man can and must remember what God has done in Jesus. Remembering, he manifests that he possesses that real life which is the gift of God, and he praises God in virtue of the life which he has received through and in Jesus. Remembering Jesus' victory over death reveals Jesus' victory over death, inasmuch as the inability to remember the wonderful works of God had characterised the condition of the dead. The eucharistic prayer of the Church praises God for his deliverance of man from the condition of death. It proclaims the new life which has been achieved through the saving death of Jesus (1 *Co* 11:20); it is existential evidence of the new life which it proclaims. Jesus has overcome man's failure to give perfect praise to God by his passion, death, and resurrection; he has overcome the condition of death by enabling mankind to participate in his perfect praise of God by the saving commemoration, remembering, of this event.

Memories Make the Future

Remembering is essential to the life of the people of God.[1] Commemoration is a Christian obligation: "Do this in commemoration of me" (*Lk* 22:19). The eucharistic celebration re-enacts Christ's sacrifice and actively expresses the Church's remembering: "This is my body which shall be given up for you; do this in remembrance of me" (1 *Co* 11:24).

Through faith, Christians share the same memories, the same history. Their sacred memories unite them as a people. For the people of God the way of recalling the past is essential for its continued existence as a community.[2] The future of the Church is promising because it remembers a past of promises: "Anyone who does eat my flesh and drink my blood has eternal life, and I shall raise him up on the last day" (*Jn* 6:54). Memories make the future. Only he can anticipate the wonderful works of the Lord, the *magnalia Dei,* who remembers them; if they are not already a part of our history, they cannot be seen as part of our future. We share in the life of the Church, the people of God, if we share its memories. We belong to a chosen people only if we remember that God has chosen us; we live in a promised land only if we remember that God had promised it. To forget this, to view the past in a different way, is to have a different history; it would be to separate ourselves from the Church and its future in the fulfilment of the promises made to it. The cohesion of the people of God perdures in shared historical memories created and sustained by faith.

There is a sense in which our memories possess us and determine what we are. An immigrant coming to the United

States, for example, has really become an American when he inadvertently remarks, "In 1776 *we* defeated the British." His new way of remembering the past indicates that he has become different; he has become an American because he now shares the memories of the American people. Similarly, Abraham becomes the father of all who, after the Spirit, share in his faith (*Mt* 3:9; *Lk* 13:16; 16:24; 19:9; *Ac* 13:26; *Rm* 11:1; *Ga* 3:29), whereas his sons according to the flesh may be disinherited (*Mt* 8:11-12; *Jn* 8:39). Even though the ancestors of most Christians had nothing to do with the history of the Hebrew people, they have all been incorporated into it through their faith in and adhesion to Christ. The God of Israel "swore an oath" with Abraham, sealed with promises (*Lk* 1:73; *Ac* 7:5-6), and Christians are the "children of the promise" (*Ga* 4:28) and its proper heirs (*Ga* 3:29). Their God is the "God of Abraham" (*Mk* 12:26; *Ac* 7:32). This same God acts on behalf of Christians; he has "glorified his servant Jesus" (*Ac* 3:13). Abraham is an essential part of Christian history: "Now if you are Christ's, then you are Abraham's seed, heirs to the promise" (*Ga* 3:26).

Existentialist insights into history help us to understand what it means to have sacred memories and lead us directly into the heart of history as a constituent of human life. Both Gabriel Marcel and Martin Heidegger have written about the meaning of care within the economy of man's existence. Every historian who cares about history organises his material around principles and events, persons and crises, about which he is interested. Historical time is structured. For Heidegger history takes its start not from the present nor from what is real only today, but from the future. The selection of what is to be an object of history is made by the historian, in whom history arises. *Man organises his past around the direction of his future.* This insight into the nature of the historian's craft has obvious implications for the way the people of God recall their sacred memories in terms of the *eschaton* and the second coming. The eucharistic commemoration is forward-looking: *"Until the Lord comes,* therefore, every time you eat this bread and drink this cup, you are proclaiming his death . . ." (1 *Co* 11:26).

Clinical psychiatry illustrates the Heideggerian insights into time in a way that deepens our appreciation of our sacred history and liturgical commemoration. The existential analyst notes that a sign of mental deterioration and psychic trauma is the patient's inability to organise the past. Even though the patient is often aware of what actually happened and capable of giving an objective account of his life, he cannot select the important and ignore the trivial; he can only record with a monotonous accuracy. His past has become a chaos because he has no future, no direction, no will to live. Time shrivels to the spatial limits of his hospital cell so that real time has departed from his life, and he is tyrannised by all-limiting space. A condition for sanity is the capacity to organise the past in the direction of the intentional thrust toward the future, a thrust which is not added to man but which constitutes him the unique being that he is. If Israel's past made sense in the light of its present under God, pointing toward a future which would transcend history, so too does the past of every sane person receive its significance in the light of his present which, like an arrow, is aimed at the future. An aimless life is not a human life; it cannot be.

Conversion illustrates the Heideggerian insight into historical time. What was once little more than a chaos of circumstance and events, the bucket of ashes which the secular mind denominates the past, suddenly coalesces and stiffens into a unity for the man blessed with the gift of faith. All sorts of random, chance events now take on a new meaning in which they are understood as having led this man to this supreme moment in which he has received the grace of God. The grace itself is a call to his future which gives meaning to his past and unifies his life into a significant whole. Our hopes, motives, and ideals stir us into action; they create our style of life, giving meaning and direction to our past.[3]

We will find in the past whatever we seek for the future. If what we seek is trivial, the past we discover will be trivial. If what we seek is noble, what we find will be splendidly human. Thus the Christian, seeking his divinisation with and in the risen Christ at the second coming and the beatific vision

146

of God, finds a past that is sacred, marvellously transcending the purely human with its wonderful works of the Lord, the *magnalia Dei*. He is tending toward the gift of God; consequently, his past is also the gift of God, a sacred memory of divine interventions in his history. The divine gift has made him capable of having this kind of history, of finding this meaning for his past. In his liturgical remembering, he recognises both his past and his future as the gift of God, anticipating the resurrection of the just in Christ and the beatific vision.

The Role of the Spirit

The Holy Spirit has a special function in the remembering of the people of God. The Church's remembering is the present fulfilment of Christ's promise to send the Holy Spirit: "The Holy Spirit, whom the Father will send in my name, he will teach you all things, and *remind* you of all that I have said to you" (*Jn* 14:26). Through the gifts of the Holy Spirit, the Father and the Son communicate the power of remembering, of sacred memories, to the people of God. The gift of the Spirit enables the Church to fulfil the command to remember: "Do this in remembrance of me" (1 *Co* 11:24). Through the gift of the Spirit the people of God adhere to Christ and his Father by actively remembering the teaching of Christ and Eucharistically commemorating his redemptive action. The trinitarian dimension of the Church's remembering appears in the fact that the Church *is* remembering, because the Father *is* sending the Holy Spirit to recall the words of Christ throughout history. Thus, love is especially attributed to the Holy Spirit, because it is through the gift of the Holy Spirit that we adhere to Christ, the Word of God, and to the Father whose reality is totally expressed by that Word. The Holy Spirit makes Christ present to us by reminding us of him, turning our minds and hearts to him. Christ is really present among the people of God because they are being *reminded* of him by his Holy Spirit, who calls their attention to his presence.

The Holy Spirit helps the Church to remember in a positive, creative way. Karl Stern, in his book *The Third Revolution*, affirms that good people who become obsessed with the evils in the world, or a particular evil, often become evil themselves. In terms of memory, they have almost lost the capacity to recall anything or anyone that was good, kind, or beautiful. The martyrs were often hated, tortured, persecuted and killed because of that to which they witnessed. The Church remembers them in a positive way which may construct a far more human future for ourselves and later generations. Hate-memories are ruled out, for the Church recalls these heroes in a way that immortalises only what was, is, and shall be forever lovable. Because the Church remembers the past with love, it can accept the future with the same spirit. Memories and visions in some way transcend time, and only the Spirit of a God who is love can empower us to transcend the malice, hatreds and inhumanity besetting us within time by remembering in a new way. Only the Spirit of God can enable us to forgive our enemies and thereby create the possibility of a new future, unpoisoned and unembittered by hate-memories. The people of God recognise that this capacity transcends the resources of human nature, and they unceasingly cry out *Veni, Creator Spiritus* on behalf of all mankind so that we may have the power to forgive and that the past may be remembered in a new way that will empower us to create a future in which all men can respect, love, and help one another as the children of God.

The Church does not bitterly recall the wickedness of those who tortured and killed its saints. It manifests its Spirit-guided historical perspective with regard to its martyrs. Its memories are not hate-memories; rather, it rejoices in the personal beauty, courage and grandeur of soul of those who preserve their identity and integrity and transcend the hatred of their persecutors. The Church liturgy officially recalls those who forgave and loved their enemies and submitted to martyrdom; it does not recall those who hated their persecutors and tried to destroy them. The people of God remember crimes committed against them in their own peculiar way: "Father, forgive them for they know not what they do." The Church prays for the "destruction" of its enemies only in the sense that they be ocnverted into friends. Only by transcending the evils and hatreds of the past through forgiveness are the people of God assured that they will transcend them in the future.

A consideration of certain aspects of remembering, as found within the biblical revelation, deepens our appreciation of the significance of remembering in Christian worship. God's remembering is our salvation, a divine gift: "Yahweh, remember me; for the love you bear your people, come to me as a saviour" (Ps 106:4). God's remembering enables our existence: "I am . . . like one forsaken among the dead, like the slain that lie in the grave, like those whom you remember no more" (Ps 88:5). His remembering manifests the power which saves Israel: "Yahweh has displayed his power, has revealed his righteousness to the nations, mindful of his love and faithfulness to the house of Israel. The most distant parts of the earth have seen the saving power of our God" (Ps 98:2-3). God's remembering is the saving power of his love: "He remembered us when we were down, his love is everlasting!" (Ps 136:23). His remembering is Israel's hope for future blessings: "Yahweh remembers us and he will bless us; he will bless the house of Israel" (Ps 115:12). His remembering reveals his mercy: "As a father pities his children, so the Lord pities those who fear him. For he knows our form: he remembers that we are dust" (Ps 103:13-14). Because God remembers her, Israel has a history. He remembers his covenant with her (Gn 9:15; Ex 2:24; 6:5; Lv 26:52; Ez 16:60; 1 Ch 16:5). His memory creates and embraces his entire relationship with his people, the *magnalia Dei* of the past as well as his concern for their future. Israel's history is the unfolding of his one eternal act of remembering.

God causes his name to be remembered at sanctuaries: "You are to make me an altar . . . In every place in which I have my name remembered I shall come to you and bless you" (Ex 20:24). God causes his works, his fidelity, and his power to be remembered:

> He allows us to commemorate his marvels.
> Yahweh is merciful and tenderhearted.
> He provides food for those who fear him;
> he never forgets his covenant.

149

He reminds his people of the power that he wields
by giving them the inheritance of the nations.

(Ps 111:4-6).

In the New Testament God continues to cause his people to
remember him. The Holy Spirit is sent to create remembrance
of Jesus and his words (*Jn* 14:26).

Throughout the Old Testament God, like Moses, David,
and Nehemiah, encourages Israel to remember. God commands Israel to "remember the sabbath day and keep it holy"
(*Ex* 20:9). The observance of the sabbath gained particular
importance after the exile and became a distinctive mark of
Judaism (*Ne* 13:15-22; 1 *M* 2:32-41); it does homage to God,
but also benefits man (*Ex* 23:12; *Dt* 5:14). God bids Israel to
keep the commandments: "You must have a tassel, then, and
the sight of it will *remind* you of all the commands of Yahweh"
(*Nb* 15:39). God loves those who remember his commandments:

> Yahweh's love for those who fear him
> lasts from all eternity and forever,
> like his goodness towards their children's children,
> as long as they keep the covenant
> and remember to obey his precepts (*Ps* 103:17-18).

Isaiah affirms Israel's obligation to remember the history
God has created for her: "Remember this and be dismayed;
stir your memories again, you sinners; remember things long
past" (*Is* 46:8). God's remembering is Israel's salvation;
Israel's remembering is her obligation. Israel's failure to
remember is sin: "And the people of Israel did not remember
the Lord their God" (*Jg* 8:34), "Our fathers refused to obey,
and forgot the wonders which you performed among them"
(*Ne* 9:17), "They forgot the God who had saved them by
performing such feats in Egypt" (*Ps* 196:21). Israel's forgetting threatens her existence as a people united by the same
memories of the *magnalia Dei*. Her continued existence hinges
upon her remembering. Israel's future was promising on the

condition that she remembered a past of promises. The promised land was meaningful only to those who remembered the promise. Israelites shared in the life of the people of God only if he shared their memories. They belonged to the chosen people only if they remembered that God had chosen them. Forgetting the past wonders of the God who had saved them would separate an Israelite from the people of God and their future. If the *magnalia Dei* are not already a part of an Israelite's history, they cannot be seen as a part of his future:

> Jerusalem, if I forget you,
> may my right hand wither!
> May I never speak again
> if I forget you,
> if I do not count Jerusalem
> the greatest of my joys (*Ps* 137:5-6).

Israel's festivals and liturgy served to activate her memory: "You shall eat no unleavened bread . . . in order that you may remember the day you came out of Egypt" (*Dt* 16:3). Israel observes the sabbath to remember the events of her liberation: "You shall remember that you were a servant in the land of Egypt, and the Lord your God brought you out with a mighty hand; *therefore* the Lord your God commanded you to remember the sabbath day" (*Dt* 5:15). The sabbath and festival days were set aside for remembering and for relating the present to the past historical interventions of Yahweh: "Remember the days of old, consider the years of many generations; ask your father, and he will show you; ask your elders, and they will tell you" (*Dt* 32:7). Memory maintains the traditions of the people of God. Observance of the sabbath represents Israel's continuing relationship with Yahweh. By remembering in the liturgical worship of the sabbath and festival days Israel gives evidence that she continues to participate in the liberating event of the historical exodus, and she makes her faithful response to the demands of the covenant (*Dt* 5:15). Thus, in Deuteronomy, Israel's remembering is an act of loving obedience to Yahweh which contrasts with her "forgetting him": "Remember Yahweh your God; it was he who gave you this strength and won you this power, thus keeping the covenant then, as today, that he swore to your fathers. Be sure that if you forget Yahweh your God, if you follow other gods, if you serve them and bow down before them — I warn you today — you will most certainly perish. Like the nations Yahweh is to destroy before you, so you yourselves shall perish, for not having listened to the voice of Yahweh your God" (*Dt* 8:18-20).

The prayers of Israel appeal to God to remember because his remembering is their salvation. Samson (*Jg* 16:28), Hannah (1 *S* 1:11), Solomon (2 *Ch* 6:42), Hezekiah (2 *K* 20:3), Nehemiah (*Ne* 1:8 and *passim*), Habakkuk (*Hab* 3:2) and Job (*Jb* 7:7 and *passim*) all plead that God remember. Jeremiah begs God to remember his covenant (*Jr* 15:15; 18:20). Israel makes the same petition (*Lm* 3:19; 5:1). The psalmist asks him to remember his people (*Ps* 25:7; 79:8; 106:4), to be mindful of his mercy (*Ps* 25:6), and to remember his Word (*Ps* 119:49), their king (*Ps* 20:3; 89:47, 50; 132:1), Israel (*Ps* 74:2), Mount Sion (*Ps* 74:2), and the day of Jerusalem against Edom (*Ps* 137:7). Moses asks him to remember the three patriarchs (*Ex* 32:13; *Dt* 9:27). The liturgical worship of Israel recalls her ancient story and the marvellous deeds of the Lord. The cult of sacred memory is a sacred reality in the life of Israel.

Memory in the New Testament

The Old Testament patterns of remembering continue into the New Testament. In the Lucan account of the crucifixion, the good thief expresses the Christian's utter dependence on the Lord's remembering as a means of his salvation, with his prayer, "Remember me, Jesus, when you come into your kingdom" (*Lk* 23:42). In the Lucan resurrection narrative, faith in the risen Lord is linked with the obligation to remember his words, when the angel commands: "*Remember* how he told you when he was still in Galilee that the Son of Man must be delivered into the hands of sinful men and be crucified, and on the third day rise' (*Lk* 24:6). The women who had come to Christ's tomb obey the command: "And *they remem-*

bered his words, and returning from the tomb they told all this to the eleven and to all the rest (*Lk* 24:8-9). Luke recognises the Lord's remembering as the grace of salvation enabling the sinner's entrance into the kingdom of God, as well as the Christian's obligation to remember the words of his Lord, as a prerequisite for communicating and participating in the mystery of the resurrection. The central act of Christian worship is a response to the divine command "Do this in commemoration of me" (*Lk* 22:19). Because the eucharistic liturgy is a commemoration not only of Christ's passion but also of his resurrection and ascension, it is characterised by the affection of joy: "Breaking bread at home, they did take their food with gladness and singleness of heart, praising God" (*Ac* 2:46). By faithfully commemorating what the risen Christ has done, Christian worshippers joyfully participate in the saving, present effects of his sacrificial action.

The Lucan parables of mercy imply the saving role of memory. The shepherd does not forget his lost sheep (*Lk* 15:4-7), the woman does not forget her lost drachma (*Lk* 15:8-10), and the father does not forget his lost son (*Lk* 15:20). They remember what has been lost and rejoice when it is found. Although Luke does not use the word for remembering, he clearly implies the redeeming power of memory which impels the shepherd to search, the woman to seek, the father to run to his son at the first sight of him, and the son to return at the recollection of his father's house. Remembering in this context is by no means passive; rather, it is the impelling, yearning force of a love which restores what has been lost.

The Lucan hymns proclaim the saving power of God's remembering.[4] Mary exclaims: "He has come to the help of Israel his servant, *mindful of his mercy* — according to the promise he made to our ancestors — of his mercy to Abraham and to his descendants forever" (*Lk* 1:54-55). Zachary sings: "Thus *he remembers* his holy covenant, the oath he swore to our father Abraham that he would grant us, free from fear, to be delivered from the hands of our enemies, to serve him in holiness and virtue in his presence, all our days" (*Lk* 1:72-75). God's remembering opens a new chapter in Israel's history. Luke describes Mary as remembering: "As for Mary, she treasured all these things and pondered them in her heart" (*Lk* 2:19), and "His mother stored up all these things in her heart" (*Lk* 2:51). Elizabeth describes her as "she who believed that the promise made her by the Lord would be fulfilled" (*Lk* 1:45). Because Mary lovingly remembers the promise — both to herself and to Abraham — she is capable of seeing its fulfilment. Her final appearance in the Lucan writings is in the fulfilment context of prayer on the eve of Pentecost: "All these joined in continuous prayer, together with several women, including Mary the mother of Jesus" (*Ac* 1:15). She is actively involved with the coming of Jesus and the Holy Spirit.

Worship expresses the gratitude of faith which remembers that the past is both the praise and the confession of God to which the people of God are admonished (*Tb* 4:5, 19; *Ex* 13:3; 1 *Ch* 16:8, 12; *Ps* 6:5). The festivals of the passover and tabernacles had been appointed for the remembrance of the past (*Ex* 12:14; 13:3; 13:9). God himself promises and faith proclaims that the divine remembrance will always be with Israel (*Ex* 3:15; *Ps* 101:12; 134:13). The divine commandments and sacrifices, the liturgical festivals and vessels foster remembrance. To assist the remembrance of the congregation, words and narratives take written form (*Ex* 17:14; *Est* 9:32). The composition of the New Testament Scriptures is an attempt to serve the remembrance of Jesus Christ and his apostles. There is a two-fold remembering in the eucharistic liturgy: the Scriptures, written that we might remember, and the eucharistic act of commemoration in the breaking of the bread.

Jesus admonishes us to remember important events of the past — "Remember Lot's wife" (*Lk* 17:32) — as well as his own words and miracles (*Mk* 8:19; *Mt* 16:9; *Jn* 15:30; 16:4). His words and actions have been for remembrance by the community. He commands it in the new act of worship he inaugurates (*Lk* 22:19; 1 *Co* 11:24-25). The liturgical eucharistic worship, in word and action, serves his remembrance.

154

Paul recognises the obligation of recalling the words of Jesus: "Remember the words of the Lord Jesus" (*Ac* 20:35). Timothy has the obligation of remembering Jesus as Paul proclaimed him: "Remember the good news that I carry: Jesus Christ risen from the dead, sprung from the race of David" (2 *Tm* 2:8). The admonition to remember embraces the word and work, life and suffering of Paul himself (1 *Th* 2:9; 2 *Th* 2:5; *Col* 4:18). The Christian community must remember its preachers, leaders and teachers: "Remember your leaders who preached the Word of God to you, and as you reflect on the outcome of their lives, imitate their faith" (*Heb* 13:7). Because Christ remains in the remembrance of the community, so also do his apostles and his messengers through whom he is remembered. The admonition to remember is a call for reflection. We were once outside Christ (*Ep* 2:11-12). Once the congregation (i.e., church of Ephesus) was blessed (*Rv* 2:5; 3:3). This remembrance should lead to acknowledgment, confession, and repentance. The command to remember demands gratitude to God and also speaks of the seriousness of the summons to repentance. Remembrance of God's saving acts as recognition, confession, and communion with God himself is seen in Hebrews 1:15, 22. Fidelity demands remembrance.

In the Emmaus account, remembering revives faith: "Then they said to each other, 'Did not our hearts burn within us as he talked to us on the road and explained the Scriptures to us?'" (*Lk* 24:32). There is a triple remembering in the Emmaus account. Jesus, the risen Lord, recalls all the passages in Scripture about himself to the Emmaus disciples (*Lk* 24:27). The disciples, after recognising Jesus in the breaking of the bread, recall their overwhelming personal experience of having had the Scriptures explained to them by Christ (*Lk* 24:32). After having recalled it for themselves, they set out for Jerusalem where they recall it for the Eleven: "Then they told their story of what had happened on the road and how they had recognised him at the breaking of bread" (*Lk* 24:35). Thus, the Emmaus encounter of the risen Christ is remembered for the benefit of the Eleven, it is remembered by the disciples themselves for their own benefit, and the passages in Scripture about the suffering of Christ are recalled by the risen Christ

155

himself for the benefit of the Emmaus disciples and their faith. The risen Christ has remembered his disciples, and their faith in him is grounded on his efficacious remembering of them and on his recalling the meaning of the Scriptures for them. Thus, faith in the risen Christ is transmitted through remembering joined with the breaking of bread. The sacred memory of the encounter with the risen Christ is the occasion for their grasping the meaning of sacred history and for their being impelled to communicate their faith to others. Something is remembered and something is done for the revival and transmission of faith in the risen Christ: Scripture and the breaking of bread. The risen Christ's remembering, in its twofold sense regarding Scripture and his disciples, is a saving grace which enables and demands our grateful remembering, a human obligation and privilege: "Do this in commemoration of me" (*Lk* 22:19). To forget this is to abandon the people of God, their sacred history, and the eschatological fulfilment of the divine promises made to them. The existence of the people of God derives from divine and human remembering.

The Emmaus account combines the declarative aspect of the traditional Jewish blessing with the eucharistic prayer. The Jews blessed God before their prayer, or request (*proseuche*). Thus, thanksgiving, based on a remembering of what God had done, preceded the prayer for his present assistance. The blessing was a grateful commemoration; the prayer following it is a hopeful petition. The Emmaus account presents Christ's recollection of God's great works and his self-revelation in the breaking of the bread. His remembering forms an integral part of an action terminating in his blessing and breaking of the bread. Similarly, the Church remembers and blesses God for the redemptive passion, death and resurrection of Christ, which constitute God's continuing blessing of the Church and the basis for its eschatological hope. Just as the Jewish blessing looked to the past in remembering and Jewish prayers looked to the future, the Church's worship is both commemorative and eschatological: "As often as you eat this bread and drink this cup, you proclaim the Lord's death until he comes" (1 *Co* 11:26).

Johannine remembering (*Jn* 14:26) involves more than a

156

mere recalling from forgetfulness or inattention. The Holy Spirit effects a realisation and a deeper insight and understanding of the words and work of Jesus. The cleansing of the temple (*Jn* 2:17; *Ps* 69:9) shows how Jesus taught his disciples to remember the Old Testament with a new understanding of it in the light of his messianic fulfilment. Only after the resurrection do the disciples remember, understand and believe the Scripture and Word which Jesus has spoken (*Jn* 2:22; 12:16). Luke also emphasises how after the resurrection the disciples remember and for the first time understand the words of Jesus. Remembering the words of Jesus is part of the Lucan Easter message (*Lk* 24:6, 8; 22:61).

The creative aspect of loving forgiveness appears in John where the breath of Jesus is a symbol of the Spirit ("breath" in Hebrew). Jesus sends forth the Spirit who will make all things anew (*Gn* 1:2; *Ez* 37:9; *Ws* 15:11; *Jn* 19:30; *Mt* 3:16): "After saying this he breathed on them and said: 'Receive the Holy Spirit. For those whose sins you forgive, they are forgiven; for those whose sins you retain, they are retained' " (*Jn* 20:22-23).

Transcending Failure through Remembering[5]

We are what we will to remember, and our memories make the future. Among some there is an ineluctable tendency to cherish only the ugliest elements that the past can offer. No degree of courtesy, friendliness, or any other form of positive change in a formerly unpleasant relationship outweighs their bitter memories, because the past they choose to remember blinds them to any good the present might offer. Their minds have become frozen with a past vision of wickedness, and the goodness or beauty of the present will remain eternally inaccessible to them.

What some Germans did several decades ago becomes the basis for suspecting all Germans today. Anti-Semitism has traditionally been based on the same principle: what a few Jews did to Christ many centuries ago became the basis for an over-riding hate-memory directed against all Jews in every age. Likewise, anti-Christian feeling among Jews has been based on the same type of hate-memory, on what some "Christians" have done to Jews. Where there is a will to hate, there is a way to sufficient evidence for hating any group. History is full of hate-evidence for the men who want it, and it continues to poison human relationships with distrust throughout the centuries.

Hate-memories perpetuate evils and human failure. The tendency to abstract only the worst of German history has produced a general apathy over German reunification. The bigot begins with the aprioristic conviction that Germans are not to be trusted and concludes that German reunification is undesirable. His security depends on the weakness of the "untrustworthy." The evidence of the past proves for this simplistic mind that Germans are basically dangerous — infact, *the* basically dangerous people. Of course, it never occurs to him that he has limited his vision to the worst elements of German history. Were he to approach French and English history, for example, in the same way, he would undoubtedly be forced to the same conclusion: the French and English are dangerous and cannot be trusted.

The hate-memory focuses on the worst of any nation's or group's past as a rationalisation for the incapacity to love others. It is a rationalisation for the inability to create personal friendship with peoples of different races, religions, classes and nations. It takes the form of the one-word definition, the unnuanced viewpoint, perpetuating hatreds for centuries and misery for millions. For this mind, "German" means Nazi, "Italian" means Mafia, "Christian" means pogrom, "Jew" means deicide, 'middle class" means hypocrisy, "Southerner" means racist, and "Negro" means crime. Friendship requires a personal creative power and effort; it is not something which just happens. The hate-memory absolves one of this responsibility.

When times are out of joint, men will be especially disposed to cross-examine the past to discover why it did not usher in a better state of affairs. The past is a kind of screen

158

upon which each generation projects its vision of the future. Historians, for example, were creating the history of the twentieth century in the very act of writing history in the nineteenth century. Similarly, each generation's judgment of the past expresses an attitude existing in the present and perduring in the future. Consequently, if the past is merely a collection of hatreds, the future can promise nothing more than the perpetuation of these hatreds. In this way, our vision of the past, whether it be our own personal past or the history of other groups, nations, races and religions, adumbrates the quality of our individual or collective future. Every man (and every society) is, therefore, responsible to future generations for the way in which he views the past. To remember only the crimes of others is to prepare a future of vendettas, reprisals and recriminations, or, at best, of tranquil hostility.

The character and humanity of the martyred Jews of our time merit far greater emphasis than the depravity of those who killed them. They died as men with faces, men who preserved their character and identity at the price of death. Had they been less gifted, less remarkable, less distinguishable from the mediocrity around them, this would never have happened to them. Inhuman perversity will martyr only the godlike, because they are a reproach to mediocrity. It would be gross to forget six million martyrs only to immortalise the hatred of those who killed them. In the long run it would only perpetuate the same destructive hatred, rather than the humanity of those who deserve remembrance. And if for Christians and Jews alike a martyr is one who dies giving witness to the one true God of all, then the six million are the martyrs of our time. For if, as we believe, the very identity of the Jewish people consists in their being the people of the Messiah, then, in some way, the six million killed for no other reason than their identity as Jews died giving witness to the one true God and his Messiah. They are the people who God has "identified," chosen, called into being. Like the Messiah, they were falsely accused and killed without cause.

As the Messiah whom Christians accept, they were also killed because of what they were, because of their identity, and they died, therefore, because of their witness to the God who had identified them as his people. And their deaths, in turn, bore witness to the one true God who, as St Paul tells us, still identifies them as his people and who will never turn his face from those whom he has eternally chosen.

Perhaps it is truer to say that men are martyred because they are saints, rather than to say that they become saints because they are martyred. They are hated, tortured, persecuted and killed because of that to which they give witness. Saints are not what the world wants, but what the world needs. The only sound way of remembering the past is a positive, constructive, human way — a way in which we may construct a far more human future for ourselves and further generations. Hate-memories will cease to produce their lethal results only when we have the good will to learn a new way of remembering, the way the people of God recall their martyrs and those who killed them. This is the way of the Spirit of God within the Church and the heart of every man of good will; it is a way of remembering which wills to recall and to immortalise only what was, is and shall be forever lovable.

Chapter 10

THE FATHER'S DELIVERANCE

The healing of mankind in Luke and Acts is initiated by the gift of the Holy Spirit, the power of God which makes Jesus the Son of God, at least in his humanity.[1] Through the agency of the Spirit and the power of God, Jesus is united to God at the deepest level of his being (*Lk* 1:35).[2]

The descent of the Spirit and the proclamation of Jesus' divine sonship constitute the central interest in the Lucan account of Jesus' baptism.[3] The Spirit and the power which are ceaselessly operative within Jesus are the Spirit and the power of the Son of God who shares in the fullness of the divine life because of his intimate relationships of "well-beloved Son" with his Father (*Lk* 3:22).[4]

Immediately after his baptism and in full possession of the power of the Spirit, Jesus confronts Satan in the desert (*Lk* 4:1-13). His healing mission involves a genuine struggle against the power of Satan, and the defeat of Satan through his suffering, death, and resurrection (*Lk* 10:13, 31; 16:11).[5] Thus, at the beginning of Jesus' public ministry (*Lk* 4:14), Luke underscores the fact that all that Jesus is about to achieve will be accomplished through the power of God in the Holy Spirit received on the day of his baptism.

Jesus sets out upon a determined mission in which his miracles will be signs of the healing which he brings.[6] He is described as "Saviour" (*Lk* 2:11; *Ac* 5:31; 13:24); he brings "salvation" (*Lk* 1:69, 71, 77; 2:30; *Ac* 28:28), a word that implies both bodily welfare and the corresponding state of spiritual health. His work, in these contexts, is related to the transformation of persons through a deliverance from the oppression of evil. Jesus heals through forgiveness, compassion, and the good news (Lk 4:18), partly expressed in his healing miracles (Lk 4:43; 9:6; 20:1). He also heals through his own suffering and death, the ultimate act of deliverance.

The power of Jesus for healing is that of the "well-beloved son"; his filial relationship with God empowers him to achieve his mission for mankind. Through the resurrection faith, his disciples believe that this is the healing relationship for mankind. Jesus is the man who had the power to address God as "Abba" and who healed sinners by authorising them to repeat this word in communion with him.[7] Jesus' abiding "Abba" relationship is that of ceaseless prayer; by sharing this relationship with mankind, he communicates the healing power of sonship with God.

Matthew viewed Jesus' healing ministry as a fulfilment of the statement in Isaiah 53:4 concerning the work of the divinely appointed Servant: "He took our sicknesses away and carried our diseases for us" (Mt 8:17). The healing of human illnesses is directly related to the work of the Servant. The Church has traditionally interpreted the Servant passages of Isaiah in terms of the atonement on Calvary. The interpretation implies that Jesus dealt also with disease and sickness on the cross as well as with human sin, and that his atonement avails for the whole personality, body as well as soul. On this basis, the Church appeals to the finished work of Jesus for physical healing as well as for spiritual restoration.

The Healing of Jesus

From the beginning of his ministry Jesus performed healing miracles (Mk 1:29-32, 40-45).[8] Luke affirms: "The power of the Lord was with him to heal" (Lk 5:17). Jesus himself affirmed that this healing power was from God (Mt 12:28; Lk 11:20). Jesus began his ministry proclaiming that healing was a sign, among others, that the rule of God, the "acceptable year of the Lord," had been inaugurated (Mt 11:5; Lk

162

4:19; 7:22). He gave his disciples authority "to heal every disease and every infirmity" (*Mt* 10:1). Their success in healing was evidence of the kingdom's nearness (*Lk* 10:9).

In some instances, Jesus attributes illness to the operation of evil in human life (*Lk* 13:16). Jesus heals the sick and diseased because it is his mission to destroy the works of the Devil. Some measure of faith is required as a condition for healing (*Mt* 9:29; *Lk* 17:19). Jesus' commitment to his Father's purpose for human wholeness and salvation (*Jn* 3:16; 10:10) is a commitment to healing the whole man.

The healing ministry of the Church is an extension of that of Jesus and his disciples.[9] Healing is a sign of the messianic age (*Ac* 2:16-21; *Jl* 2:28-31). Peter, Paul, and Philip engage in healing work (*Ac* 3:11; 5:15; 8:9-13). This work is linked to the forgiveness of sins (*Jm* 5:16). Faith in the person of Jesus (*Ac* 3:6), prayer and anointing with oil (*Jm* 5:14; cf. *Mk* 6:13), and the "laying on of hands" (*Ac* 9:12) all belong to the healing process. The process, however, is initiated by the gift conferred by the Holy Spirit (1 *Co* 12:10, 28) — the Spirit given by the risen Christ (*Ac* 2:33), and through whose power, as sons in the Son, we can pray "Abba, Father" (*Rm* 8:15; *Ga* 4:6). Jesus heals by sharing his relationship to the Father with others; it is only after the resurrection that Jesus becomes the donor of the Spirit through whom this healing relationship is achieved (*Ac* 2:33).

St Paul twice says that it is proof of the possession of sonship and of the Spirit when a Christian repeats the one word "Abba." The ancient Christian liturgies manifest their awareness of the greatness of this gift in that they preface the Lord's Prayer with the words: "We *make bold* to say: 'Our Father.' "[10] This formal liturgical prayer articulates that healing and abiding relationships to the Father which the Christian has received through the Spirit of Jesus as a gift of which he stands in ceaseless need and for which he is ceaselessly grateful. A a son derives his life from his father, the Christian derives his life from the Father of Jesus, through participation in Jesus' ceaseless relationship of sonship as expressed by "Abba."

The Chritian recognises that his health, healing, and salvation come from a source outside himself; he is ceaselessly in need of that life which transcends his own resources and heals his infirmities. Just as Jesus invoked his Father in the great crisis of his life, the Christian does likewise; however, in the case of both Jesus and the Christian, the intense prayers of crisis well up from an abiding and ceaseless attitude of trust and filial love. This attitude or state of soul corresponds somewhat to what the dogmatic theologian might describe as sanctifying grace and the theological virtues of faith, hope, and charity; it suggests what the moral theologian might call the fundamental option for God. In any case, it is always a gift, a healing gift empowering a ceaseless turning to God in an ongoing *metanoia,* praise, petition, and thanksgiving for what he is accomplishing through his Son's healing mission.

The healing mission of Jesus is accomplished through his filial dependence upon God. Jesus requires the same continuing attitude of dependence from his disciples, telling them about the need to pray always and never to lose heart (*Lk* 18:1). Paul's "Pray always" (1 *Th* 5:17) also assumes that prayer is a constant of Christian living.

The meaning of Jesus' healing mission, like that of any process, emerges in its term. The way in which Jesus accomplishes his Father's work of healing and of reconciling man with God, his neighbour, and himself emerges at the term of Jesus' life with his exclamation on the cross: "It is finished." The character of his healing life emerges in that paradoxical event which is both an outward failure and an inward victory. Jesus has failed to convert Israel by his preaching; however, he has succeeded in accomplishing his Father's will. His prayer, "Abba, forgive them, for they know not what they do" (*Lk* 23:34), articulates his life-long spirit of loving and healing intercession on behalf of mankind. His dying prayer is an implicit interpretation of his entire life.

At the institution of the eucharist, Jesus had said that his death would be "for many" (*Mk* 14:24). His prayer of intercession on the cross applies the atoning power of his death to his executioners, recalling the healing mission of the Servant

164

of the Lord (*Is* 53:12) who made intercession for his transgressors by voluntarily, patiently, and innocently undergoing death in accordance with God's will (*Is* 53:6-10).

The Cross as a Sign of Liberation

Through the experience of the resurrection-faith, the disciples no longer view Calvary as a catastrophe. They now see the cross as their source of peace, joy, and liberation. The self-emptying, self-giving, self-transcending work of Jesus produces its healing effect by completely changing the attitude of the disciples toward the outward failure of Calvary. The disciples have a radically new understanding of Jesus' death and of death in general; they have been enlightened and transformed by the prayerful suffering and death of Jesus. They now share in that peace and joy which exist first in God, obtained by Jesus' death, and they understand that this is to enter into Jesus' kingdom of heaven.[11]

The passion account presents in intensified form some aspects of Jesus' filial obedience to his Father's work of healing. The "Abba" relationship of Jesus to his Father is especially prominent in the incident of the agony in the garden, which stands at the beginning of the passion drama much as the story of the temptations stands at the beginning of Jesus' public ministry. Jesus obediently responds to his Father's loving will to heal mankind and is "delivered up according to the definite plan and foreknowledge of God" (*Ac* 2:23).

The incident of the agony in the garden reveals both Jesus' human abhorrence of death and his Father's will as the basic reason for his acceptance of his passion and death. The intense prayer of the garden, arising from his abiding "Abba" relationships, ends with the transformation of Jesus' feelings toward his death. Voluntary and peaceful acceptance, rather than natural dread, governs Jesus' subsequent action. His dread of death seems to have been overcome in what is apparently a healing effect of his own prayer.

Ultimately, the cross is the victory of the Father's healing love in Jesus, delivering man from everything he most fears.

His gift of perfect love in Jesus casts out all human fears; it is perfectly expressed in Jesus, the New Adam, in whom man is revealed as finally healed and delivered from evil. Through the "Abba" relationship of Jesus to his Father, death has been transformed into the healing and deliverance of mankind.

The risen Christ is the New Adam — man as perfectly reconciled with that Love which transcends all evils, even death itself.[12] He who has fully received the Father's transcendent love is empowered by that love to transcend all evils, even death itself. This is announced as the good news, the kind of healing that is achieved through suffering and death: "Was it not necessary that the Christ should suffer these things and enter into his glory?" (*Lk* 24:26). Jesus' filial obedience achieves a victory over all those tendencies in human nature which run counter to a relationship of perfect sonship with God. Evil is overcome by the love of the Father in the Son as reconciling, and by the love of the Son whose self-giving embraces both the Father and man, and so links both anew. The healing Spirit of the Son communicates that love which empowers man to love what God loves. Healing reconciles man's will with God's call to him. Through the Father's self-giving in Jesus and the Holy Spirit, man is a participant in the creative love of God for his neighbour, for himself, and for the entire world.[13]

The healing that Jesus accomplished on the cross culminates the historical dimension of his "Abba" relationship. The accomplishment cannot be understood apart from the life which it ended, the life which incarnated God's self-giving mode of being in the world for the world's reconciliation with the love that brought it into existence.

The cross does not represent Jesus' attempt to change God. It is not an historical event necessary for God to be able to accept man.[14] This view is avoided by recalling Jesus' own parable of the prodigal son who finds the father willing to receive him, though there is no special method to make possible a reconciliation (*Lk* 15:11-32). The first step toward reconciliation is taken when the son becomes aware of the disorder of his own existence. His awareness of sin initiates

166

his turning away from it. Insight leads to conversion. The father does not need to be placated. Before the son came to his senses, the father was already awaiting and desiring his return. He sees him at a distance and is already on his way to meet him and bring him home. The parable stresses the unchanging character of God's attitude and work, which is always one of reconciliation.

Although it was necessary that some particular historical event should reveal in a signal way "the mystery hidden for ages and generations," no historical event changes God's attitude or turns him from a wrathful God into a gracious God. The historical work of Jesus is identical with the eternal self-giving love of his Father, whose effects are revealed in Jesus and all those who are being healed through him.

The Father's establishment of the "Abba" relationship in and through Jesus heals mankind of its root sin of idolatry.[15] Speaking of the perversion of man's life through sin, St Paul points to idolatry as the source of the trouble: "They exchanged the truth about God for a lie and worshipped and served the creature rather than the Creator" (*Rm* 1:25).

To worship an idol is to make an ultimate concern of something that is not ultimate; the only possible result must be a terrible distortion of human existence. Idolatry is the effort to understand life and give it meaning in terms of finite beings, to the exclusion of God. The effort to found life upon creatures, perhaps man himself, rather than God estranges man from his true being, from his neighbour, and from God.

St Paul portrays the cross as the battle against the demons that afflict the life of man. The cross overcomes these demonic, enslaving powers by establishing the "Abba" relationship. St Paul asserts that God "has delivered us from the kingdom of darkness and transferred us to the kingdom of his beloved Son" (*Col* 1:13). Through the healing "Abba" relationship of Jesus, God has abolished the claim of these dark powers over us: "This he set aside, nailing it to the cross" (*Col* 2:14). Through Jesus' perfect expression of sonship, man has been delivered: "He disarmed the principalities and powers and made a public example of them, triumphing over them" (*Col* 2:15).

167

The vanquished demonic powers are linked with the root sin of idolatry. To worship an idol is to give it demonic power. In man's quest for fulfilment, idolatry can lead only to the stunting and distorting of the self (*Ps* 115:8). The idolatrous self is inhibited from growth; it is a travesty of the *imago Dei* that it was intended to be. Pride is an expression of man's idolising of himself and his powers; it perverts relations among men. When man idolises himself, he becomes his own god and paves the way for his alienation from others. Greed, lust, and other forms of degrading self-indulgence express man's self-destructive tendency to idolise things. Pride, lust, and greed are ultimately forms of idolatry, a turning away from God to creatures.

The Old Testament also identifies idols with demons: "They sacrificed to demons which were no gods, to gods they had never known, to new gods that had come in of late, whom your fathers had never reverenced. You were unmindful of the Rock that begot you, and you forgot the God who gave you birth" (*Dt* 32:17f.). This is precisely the forgetting of God, the exaltation of creatures above the Creator, an idolatrous worship of the beings which in turn have enslaved us and react upon us with demonic effect.

Luke's Gospel emphasises the completeness of the power of God and the Spirit of Jesus in connection with the temptation in the desert (*Lk* 4:1-13), and so brings the struggle with the demonic forces within the scope of Jesus' divine mission.[16] Victory over these forces, as well as the exercise of wisdom and judgment, was part of the work of the Spirit-possessed messianic leader prophesied by Isaiah (*Is* 11:1-5). One aspect of the victory appears when Jesus rejects the temptation to make worldly power his ultimate concern, because this is equated with worshipping Satan.

Throughout his career, Jesus will not enslave himself to any idol; he acknowledges only the Father's authority in his attitude of filial dependence and responsiveness. His refusal to idolise any being, whether worldly beings or his own being or mankind, reveals the freedom that ultimately enables all men to become the sons of God, for the "Abba" relationship that

168

characterises the life and death of Jesus is the Father's victory over man's fatal tendency to idolatry. Refusal to idolise any created being is to deprive it of any possibility of acquiring demonic power over us. Jesus breaks the dominion of the demons and puts them to flight by giving himself utterly in the passion and death of the cross.

Central to the passion and death of Jesus is his self-giving. If one's own self is the last idol, then to give even oneself unreservedly is to have become like God and to have vanquished the last demon. Jesus' self-giving overcomes those evils which are so great that man calls them demonic, for they are beyond his control. Man attempted to live independently of his Creator, treating himself as his own god, and he thereby not only ceased to be truly himself but also lost control of what should have been under his dominion and fell under the sway of the demonic powers, the powerful values of the created universe which should be his servants for the glorification of God. Through the cross they are returned to their proper status and function. When Jesus as man becomes Lord over all things, these are not annihilated but reduced to their proper service to the Father, and to mankind, through participation with Jesus in his "Abba" relationship.

Jesus gained his title of Lord by his self-humiliation and filial obedience; he freely accepted the status of man, the way of life God created for him, and showed no anxiety to share the status of God (*Ph* 2:5-11). Therefore, he was rewarded for faithful sonship by being made the head of all creation; to him every knee bows, of things in heaven, on earth, and under the earth. This recalls the fact that as a result of his sin Adam lost the lordship over creation he was intended to have and became the subject of heavenly, earthly, and nether powers. Man's true existence is evidenced by the filial obedience and the exaltation of Jesus, and through this reaches the dominion promised to man in creation (*Gn* 1:28). He also exercises a further lordship over the rest of men as the first-born among many brethren (*Rm* 8:29).

The cross runs counter to man's will-to-power, his impatience with a position suggesting any kind of inferiority. If,

169

by throwing off the yoke of filial service to God, man lost his own proper authority over all else in creation, with and for which he was created, it is by the establishment of the "Abba" relationship in the cross that Jesus regains it. The self-seeking and the self-centred desire that had led Adam to turn his back on God is undone by the power of the cross through which man returns to the Father (1 *Co* 1:18).

Death as a Continuation, Not an End

Jesus' death must be recognised as continuous with his life; it is the signal climax by which his healing work is completed in opening up a new possibility of existence, an existence oriented toward God, sustained by the self-giving love of God, and communicating and sharing this love with others. The culminating providential work of God in the passion, death and resurrection of Jesus establishes and sustains man in the face of the threat of his disintegration through idolatry's misplaced commitment.

The self-giving of Jesus on Calvary is continuous with that of his Father; it brings his Father's self-giving for man into the very life of the New Adam, the new man, Jesus of Nazareth, the unique sign of the "Abba" relationship that is at the core of his existence.

The self-emptying spirit of the "Abba" relationship overcomes the dehumanising tendency to self-glorification and self-idolising. Jesus affirms that the glory which really counts is that which we receive from God: "If I were to seek my own glory, that would be no glory at all; my glory is conferred by the Father" (*Jn* 8:54). The "Abba" relationship is an abiding participation in the absolute truth and glory that is the Father's. Hence, self-righteousness, self-seeking, self-affirmation, and self-glorification are forms of idolatry that reject the call to share in the "Abba" relationship of Jesus; they preclude the experience of the healing enlightenment, love, and peace that derives from the Father's self-giving in Jesus.

Creator and creature are at one in the achievement of the cross. The self-giving of God occurs in the self-emptying of

Jesus, the way that the Word of God has become incarnate, the way that God heals, enlightens, and reconciles mankind. Jesus, tempted like other men, yet "obedient unto death, even death on a cross" (*Ph* 2:8), achieves the divine work of reconciliation with a cooperation that is fully human. We see in Jesus the destiny that God has set before humanity; he is the first fruits, but the Christian hope is that through his "Abba" relationship with God all men will be brought to full reconciliation and divine sonship.

Jesus' experience of failure in his historical mission to convert Israel is that of a free man for whom adherence to the truth of his mission is more important than the "success" of his mission.[17] The power of his adherence to the truth of his "Abba" relationship to his Father will ultimately be vindicated by a faith-realisation among his disciples that the undergoing of the suffering and death of the cross in the experience of failure was the effective means of the Divine Wisdom for transforming mankind by the realisation and experience of what Jesus was all about. The joyful and liberating experience of incorporation into Jesus' "Abba" relationship with God convinces the disciples of the power and appropriateness of the means chosen by the Divine Wisdom for the healing and deliverance of mankind.

The Gospels do not speculate about the other possible ways in which the Father might have successfully communicated the relation of sonship to mankind. They are too excited about the wondrous way in which thousands of human lives have been radically transformed; they communicate the conviction that there was no better means than the cross for the accomplishment of man's deliverance and transformation; they implicitly witness their incorporation into the "Abba" relationship by their conviction that the cross is the Father's will and way of liberation for those who are his sons in the Son; they share the conviction of Jesus in the garden of olives that the cross is the Father's means for the achievement of his work. The cross is seen as a creative conflict with all those powers of evil that had precluded anything like an "Abba" relationship with God; it has created new men, vindicating the power of Jesus' freedom in loving obedience and sonship over all the forces of ultimate

171

failure. The work of Jesus has empowered a change of direction by delivering man and his society from the enslaving demonic forces of self-idolisation and other forms of idolatry. The work of the cross is a work of grace that lays hold on the human race through the irrevocable establishment of an historical and eternal, healing and transforming "Abba" relationship between man and God.

The martyrs and saints bear witness to the self-giving and self-emptying love of Jesus that is operative in their lives. The Church believed that the martyrs had no need of purgation because by utterly giving themselves they had attained the fullest potentialities of their existence, inasmuch as they utterly transcended selfishness and achieved a likeness to Christ and his Father.[18] The Church eventually recognised that there are ways of self-transcendence, of self-renunciation and of self-denial other than giving oneself to physical death that may be to no less a degree the expression of the same love that was in Jesus.

The martyrs and saints bear witness to the reality of God's sanctifying work in the world. Their self-giving, self-emptying love committed them to a future in which they had to lose themselves in order to transcend themselves and communicate the kingdom of God. The communion of saints participates in the ceaseless prayer of Jesus which sanctifies the world and heals its infirmities. All Christians belong to this fellowship in which the work of sanctification is going on; however, the character of the fellowship is especially manifest in those who have attained such a degree of sanctification as to be recognised by the community as a whole. The meaning of Jesus' work of reconciliation and healing is witnessed by the saints.

The process of sanctification and healing is expressed in such sayings as that one must "die to live" and that "whoever would save his life will lose it, and whoever loses his life for my sake and the Gospel's will save it" (*Mk* 8:35). Sanctification and healing represent the genuine fulfilment of selfhood. The contrast between the fulfilment attained by self-transcendence and the illusory fulfilments sought within the narrow limits of self-regarding concern is expressed in the question:

"What does a man gain by winning the whole world at the cost of his true self?" (*Mk* 8:36).

Through participation in the "Abba" relationship of Jesus we look beyond the limits of our own self, finitude, transience, and mortality for the master concern of our existence; we transcend the superficiality of those ambitions on which human energies are wasted in the quest for an illusory security; we avoid the self-distortion that comes from making pleasure or self-aggrandisement the leading concern of our life. In these and many other ways we are healed by an on-going participation in the "Abba" relationship; we are liberated from the obstacles that our various forms of idolatry put in the way of any genuine love for God and neighbour.

Our participation in the "Abba" relationship implies a self-understanding which is born of a religious faith in those resources beyond our own to help us to fulfil the claims that our very existence lays upon us. It implies abiding filial qualities: fidelity to the self-giving Love that brought us into existence, sustains our existence, and promises existence even more fully; gratitude for and remembrance of the event which established and revealed this filial relationship; joy in the present awareness of our participation in the Father's life; hope and expectation of our complete assimilation into this life, and a constant dying to ourselves in the process of becoming the self which is to fulfil the promise of God.

Prayer and Healing

The "Abba" relationship implies an attitude of ceaseless prayer: a continuous responsiveness to the transcendent, the holy, the reality of realities, the one without counterpart, the eternal truth, the divine, and all that is meant by what we call God and what Jesus called "Abba"; an on-going receptiveness to that divine reality which, although transcendent, is also immanent in our hearts, nearer than our very pulse, more inward than our innermost being; an abiding awareness of the

173

supreme beauty, goodness, righteousness, and truth; an awareness that nothing in the world of nature or spirit can be compared to this reality, the final goal of all longing and striving, experienced as outgoing and all-encompassing love, as the great heart of compassion and forgiveness.

The "Abba" relationship implies an abiding love of neighbour, even enemies. It implies a fraternal love without limitations, love that has its source not in man himself but in God operating on man, a love that, as it comes from God, also returns to him, for in loving our neighbour we are loving God. The "Abba" relationship is a filial love for the Father, so that ultimate happiness is conceived as the knowledge or vision of him, as union with him, or as dissolution into him.

Sharing the "Abba" relationship with Jesus implies a way of healing through self-sacrifice, renunciation, and resignation. The "Abba" relationship may be expressed partly in words, partly without words, partly in complete solitude, partly in the community of those who share the same relationship. It is a whole life of seeking God himself and his rule on earth; hence, it involves our dying to ourselves that Abba in Jesus may live in us and thereby become our deliverance and healing.

The genuine healing power of ceaseless prayer is affirmed by the New York psychiatrist, Dr. Thomas Hora, in his informally published notes (Chapter 7, "Prayer," pp. 85-95).[20] Dr. Hora's affirmations generally corroborate, from the standpoint of psychiatry, our theological reflections on the healing character of our participation in the "Abba" relationship of Jesus, that dynamic relationship radically transforming those who accept it. The following is a resume of Dr Hora's view on ceaseless prayer and its healing power.

Ceaseless prayer is described as a continuous mode of being and a way of life, motivated by a hunger and thirst for understanding the truth of Existence, the truth of God, his universe, and man's place in it. It is a loving, reverential, responsive, and cognitive mode of being in the world. It is reverential because it is receptive. It is responsive because it does not originate in man. It is cognitive because it takes place in man's conscious-

174

ness. It is existential worshipping, or prayer in action and underlying action.

The condition of man's consciousness reveals itself by the quality of his presence in the world. A consciousness which is in harmony with Existence, which reverences the will of God and his fundamental order of being, reveals itself as a loving, intelligent, beneficial presence. Such a presence lives and moves and has its being in a relatively friendly world where obstacles, problems, and difficulties are encountered with a spirit of peace and wisdom. What a man thinks in his heart, according to Dr. Hora, tends to determine his way of experiencing life, as well as the way in which others will experience him. A man inevitably communicates what he loves. These are his abiding concerns. Whatever, therefore, attracts or captures our abiding concern becomes our god; hence, Dr. Hora concludes that man is an eminently prayerful creature with a large choice of gods that he can worship. The question of prayer is not whether to pray or not to pray, but what to pray to and how.

The secret gods which man treasures in the secrecy of his fantasies, daydreams, yearnings and fears become manifest in the quality of his presence in the world and thus in turn shape his experience and his future. Our abiding concerns (whether idols or the true God) shape our character, so we tend to become what we worship. Finding the true God to worship is the problem. Public worship, depending on its quality, can be a support in finding the right God to worship.

A beneficial presence is an indication of our having found the right God to worship. The quality of our presence is determined by our prayers. A beneficial presence benefits everyone with whom it establishes contact, even without any intentional verbal communication. There are people who are a joy to all who are near them. Their presence is a blessing to an entire household or group, even to an entire community. Dr. Hora believes that somehow their beneficial consciousness tends to spread and harmonise the affairs of people in a large area. Their presence is a type of beneficial intercessory prayer inasmuch as they are in communion with that self-giving divine Love-Intelligence which is *the* beneficial presence for the entire

175

universe. There is no other way for a man to be a genuinely beneficial presence in the world.

Ceaseless prayer to the one, true God results in a genuinely beneficial presence through which limitless possibilities of good enter into human experience, both individually and collectively. It is through such ceaseless prayer that the process of healing individuals and society takes place and the peace of God becomes the reconciliation of man with himself, his neighbour and his God.

Only he who has health, for Dr. Hora, can communicate health. Ultimately, God alone is good and the source of healing for the human heart and society. Prayer is the effective relationship of the healed to the Healer; a beneficial presence is empirical evidence of this relationship. Man shares in God's healing work to the extent that God has healed him; man shares in God's beneficial presence to the extent that he benefits from that presence.

Dr. Hora explains how the genuine worship of God in the state of ceaseless prayer heals man. He explains that it turns the human spirit away from its false assumptions, false values, erroneous and superficial concerns, and misdirected and harmful orientations. It purifies the human spirit by turning it away from a mental content that impedes or diminishes its awareness of the presence of God, of his peace and his loving self-giving. Through prayer the mind is purified and enlightened; it reflects with the spirit of love that is beneficial to man. Sound mental health, for Dr. Hora, is ultimately a question of the quality of man's ceaseless prayer.

Effective prayer implies a level of wholeness. The more wholesome we are, the more wholesome we can become. Dr. Hora subscribes to a law of spiritual growth or healing according to which the man who possesses considerable wholesomeness will tend to a greater wholesomeness than his fellow man who is less wholesome. Goodness is not static; it grows. The greater the goodness, the greater the momentum of its beneficial growth and the impact of its beneficial presence. Ceaseless prayer is a process of growth and development which inevitably leaves its residue in human society.

The process of healing also involves the human inclination to become absorbed with either the sensuous, emotional, or intellectual level of his existence, or to fluctuate among these three levels, without ever transcending them for a higher experience of life. As the human spirit becomes liberated from the overwhelming concern with its own comfort and well-being, it begins to lose interest in the many supportive means designed to assure its satisfaction of this concern. It recognises that feeling good is more a result of being good rather than an artificial state induced by man-made stimuli. For genuine wholesomeness and a wholesome feeling, man must be concerned about being good rather than just feeling good. Dr. Hora warns that the quest for feeling good, when it becomes a primary concern, is often really destructive of health. Genuine ceaseless prayer introduces a shift in concern, a conversion, from personal comfort to personal wholesomeness; it introduces a shift in concern from feeling good to being a beneficial presence in the world. Seeking the kingdom of God and its righteousness is the wholesome, healing activity whose by-product is the feeling of cosmic all-rightness, harmony with God and his world.

Psychiatry, Dr Hora believes, sheds some light on the nature of intercessory prayer. In some cases Dr Hora maintains that the child can be healed only by the healing of the mother. She must become a channel of love which is not possessive but liberating. She might talk to her child endlessly to solve his problem and it would do no good because what she says has no healing effect unless it is fully expressive of what she is. The mother must first become free of her life-long habit of possessiveness. She must realise that her child is not absolutely hers, that it belongs to God and that it always has belonged to God. When she understands that she is the custodian of God's child, it becomes possible for her to love without possessiveness. A child, once released from his parents' possessiveness, can grow freely without anxiety at times of separation from his parents. Separation anxiety is overcome with the realisation that we are always living, moving, and having our being in God. This case illustrates how the healing of one person is contingent upon the healing of another. The improvement of others may require our own improvement as a condition, as a type of efficacious intercessory prayer.

In the relationship of mother and child, Dr Hora notes that the quality of the mother's presence is transmitted to the child directly. The child will inevitably reflect whether it is being loved possessively or freely. If it is being loved possessively, the child will tend to be aggressive and possessive; if it is being loved freely, it will tend to be peaceful and receptive.

The beneficial quality of a man's presence illuminates one aspect of intercessory prayer. Such a presence implies the wholeness of a loving person and the elimination of selfishness. Dr Hora observes that even the quality of silence has been changed within families when one member overcomes selfishness to become a beneficial presence; this has occurred because the quality of that member's consciousness has changed.

There are many shadings of the qualities of presence. The quality of presence may be obtrusive, overbearing, hostile, depressing, joyous, exciting, inspiring, seductive, healing, and so on. In fact, Dr Hora notes that the presence of some is an absent one. Our future depends largely on our social relations, and these are constituted in large measure by the quality of our presence. This is what people respond to. Through the authentic worship of ceaseless prayer, Dr Hora believes that man is enabled to share in the transcending consciousness of God's self-giving love and wisdom; this enables man to live a life of intercessory prayer, a life which Dr Hora understands as the beneficial, loving radiancy reaching out of one human consciousness for the welfare of another. Such consciousness communicates a loving climate in society. It is the consciousness of a mind that has been liberated (healed) from an overwhelming concern with its own comfort, security, and wellbeing. Authentic worship in the state of ceaseless prayer is the ultimate basis for the health of man and society.

The yoke of Jesus (*Mt* 11:29f), according to Dr Hora, makes life easy to bear because it implies a life permeated by

178

the loving consciousness of the Father's healing, self-giving presence in a universe where everything works for the good (healing) of those who love him. This quality of consciousness is the gift of God which alleviates our burdens and those of others; it grounds our abiding attitude of ceaseless prayer and our desire to share in Jesus' loving, self-giving, beneficial presence in the world.

The Church as the body of Christ participates in the ceaseless prayer that characterises Jesus' filial relationship to his Father. The Holy Spirit of Jesus informs and inspires the worship of the Church. It is the worship offered by the children of God, by those to whom Jesus has given access to the Father, by those who are born of the Spirit (*Jn 3:5*). It is the worship offered by the sons of God with the Spirit through whom the sonship has been imparted. The prayer of the Church effectively prolongs the historical impact of Jesus' healing prayer relationship with his Father. The principle *lex orandi lex credendi,* the law of worship, is not mere liturgical rule; it is the abiding state of the Church in worship, in the very act of union with the Father through the ceaseless prayer of Jesus here and now. It is the state of being healed and of healing others.

The *Pastoral Constitution on the Church in the Modern World* recognised the on-going character of Jesus' healing work through the gift of his Spirit within the Church. "For it is the function of the Church, led by the Holy Spirit who renews and purifies it ceaselessly, to make God the Father and his incarnate Son present and in a sense visible" (n. 21). The healing process communicates the presence of the Healer. The same Constitution implies that it is a beneficial presence: "This faith needs to prove its fruitfulness by penetrating the believer's entire life, including its worldly dimensions, and by activating him toward justice and love, especially regarding the needy. What does most to reveal God's presence, however, is the brotherly charity of the faithful who are united in spirit as they work together for the faith of the Gospel and who prove themselves a sign of unity" (n. 21). It concludes that everyone ought to communicate a beneficial presence by working

179

for the rightful betterment of the world in which he lives (n. 21). The transformation of the world is the intercessory aspect of Jesus' and the Church's "Abba" relationship to the Father. It is a dynamic relationship healing its authentic participants through the Father's deliverance from evil.

AFTERWORD

LESS THAN THREE WEEKS after the election of Pope Francis, *Corriere della Sera* (29th March 2013) published Armando Torno's article about the major influences on the thought of the new pope. Immediately after St Theresa of Avila, Pope Francis mentioned the theology of failure of the Italian-American Jesuit John Navone, commenting that the Christian faith does not promise an exemption from failure, but rather a way of dealing with it advantageously; that even the mission of Christ, judged by mere human standards, seemed to culminate in total failure. The following day, Matteo Matzuzzi, covering the influences on the new pope in *Il Foglio* stated that 'He adores the theology of failure of the Jesuit John Navone.'

Pope Francis, in the book of his conversations with Sergio Rubin and Francesca Ambrogetti (*Papa Francesco: Il Nuevo Papa Si Racconta*, Milano: Salani Editore, 2013, p. 65) had already made reference to my theology of failure: 'Patience is a theme that I have pondered for years, after my having read the book of John Navone, an Italian-American author ' with the striking title. *The Theology of Failure*, in which he explains how Jesus lived patiently. Patience is forged in the experience of limits. There are times when our lives do not call so much for our doing as for enduring, for bearing up with our own limitations and those of others. Patience accepts the fact that it takes time to develop and mature. Living with patience allow for time to integrate and shape our lives' (My translation).

Curiously enough, the English translation of this book describes me merely as 'an Italian author,' apparently no longer either American or Jesuit, and utterly anonymous!

Pope Francis had read the Italian translation (1978) of my theology of failure, which had been published by Paulist Press in New York in 1974. That, after thirty-five years he should publicly affirm the book's impact on his thought amazed me; for even though we are both Jesuits, and of Italian parentage, we had never met.

Too many people are crippled by fear or failure, thinking that they are failures in experiencing failure when they have, in fact, not failed to give their lives for the right cause. Mark's Gospel's very structure shows a radical turning point in the mission of Jesus. Although tremendously popular in the first half of the Gospel, Jesus stops working miracles midway in the Gospel and becomes progressively unpopular with everyone, starting with his own family, relatives, disciples, religious and political authorities turning away from him until he dies with no Mary or John at the foot of the cross as a total failure without seeing billions of Christians applauding him. The structure of Mark's Gospel tells us Jesus did not live for popularity, success, fame, glory; in fact, the more he proceeds to the accomplishment of his Father's will, the more unpopular he becomes, the more he 'fails' to be a crowd-pleaser. His story, contrary to the common view of what-did-we do-wrong-to-deserve-this, tells us that people are just as often hated, despised and killed because of their excellence which has become an unbearable reproach to unscrupulous individuals, groups and societies. The Resurrection reveals God's approval of the object of human disapproval. As the father of lies, Satan the Adversary reigns where persons and nations live for self-glorification in a state of self-idolatry, persons whose very lives secrete a life-lie. The conflict between Jesus and the religious authorities can be understood in terms of what authority means: the ability to 'author' something of true value in others. , Jesus authored an authentically religious/godly life that clashed with that of the pseudo-religious authorities. He condemned the pretentiousness, self-righteousness and self-glorification of a specious religiousness whose practitioners he denounced as "whitened sepulchers... Jesus denounces them for failing to embody and communicate the authentic meaning and value of their religious heritage.

Fear of failure too often condemns us to mediocrity. It is suicidal for many an incipient hero. The motto of such fear is 'better a live jackass than a dead lion.' Such crippling fear is often motivated by cowardice. Hans Christian Andersen tells of people who are afraid to tell the monarch he is naked. Paradoxically, fear of failure is often succumbing to failure itself. Would there have been the Resurrection had Jesus feared human failure? I believe most great human achievements

182

have been made by persons who successfully overcame the fear of human failure.

Our encounter with failure raises the question of whether we are prepared to serve God only in success. If so, our service of God ultimately becomes a form of self-service, of self-will, as opposed to God's will. We must learn to do God's will out of love for God and not for our own fame or satisfaction. God permits our failures to educate us, leading us to better choices. Human failures are never outside the realm of God's saving providence. They can lead us to learn from the wisdom of others rather than succumb to the hubris of relying entirely on ourselves. Failure is often God's deliverance from the illusion of self-sufficiency, believing more in ourselves than in God.

FAITH AND FREEDOM: A JOURNAL OF PROGRESSIVE RELIGION, PUBLISHED AT HARRIS MANCHESTER COLLEGE, OXFORD, ENGLAND

SPRING AND SUMMER 2014

Editor's Note: The following address was given on April 24th by Father James Schall at Gonzaga University (Spokane, WA), at the invitation of the school's Faith and Reason Institute, in honor of Father John Navone, SJ.

"REMEMBERING ONE'S TRADITION IS at the heart of both the Jewish and Christian identity. Israel's remembering is essential for her continued existence as God's covenant people, forgetting God's saving acts would bring her destruction. 'You shall remember the Lord your God...that he may confirm his covenant which he swore to your fathers, as at this day. And if you forget the Lord our God...I solemnly warn you that you shall surely perish' (Deut. 8: 18-10). Through her remembering, Israel's redemptive history continues in a living tradition

where the divine commands perdures as historical events challenging successive generations to decision and that obedience which enables Israel to share in the redemption of here forefathers."
— Father John Navone, SJ, "No Tradition, No Civilization", Homiletic & Pastoral Review, October, 2002.

I.

The most memorable passage that I recall from many years of knowing Father John Navone, of corresponding with him, and of reading him is the following: "You are what you remember." Whether this insightful sentence is unique to John Navone, I do not know, but he often used it. I have cited it many times myself, or, in a similar spirit: "Tell me what you remember, and I will tell you what you are." From this angle of remembrance, I will approach my appreciation of John Navone's work. "To remember" implies the existence of time and its passing-ness. From there it gets us to tradition and history.

These considerations lead us, not to deadly "timelessness," but rather to eternity, to the nuc stans, to the "now" that stands in hushed stillness, as Aquinas put it. The reason that the silence, the stillness, is hushed is because this is our first reaction to seeing something of immeasurable, or even measurable, beauty. Beauty is a prominent theme of John Navone. He talks about "remembering" because he thinks that something to remember is constantly before us. The classic definition of beauty was: Quod visum, placet—"What is seen or heard pleases us." This capacity to be pleased by anything is one of the most curious things about us. We not only encounter lovely things, but they please us, delight us, as if we are made both to receive and to acknowledge the glory of what we have received, of what is not ourselves

In an article by Julie Krug in Spokane's Spokesman-Review (June 21, 2008), Father Navone, recalling the Spokane part of his early education, remarked: "It was at Mt. St. Michael's here in Spokane, with its superb instructors, that I began to study philosophy and learned about what I call 'The Life of the Mind.'" In 2006, ISI Books published a book of Schall's entitled, precisely: The Life of the Mind: On the Joys and

Travails of Thinking. I had no idea at the time that I was echoing John Navone, due, no doubt, to a loss of memory! But Navone was right. The instructors at Mt. St. Michael's in our time were superb. I was in the class ahead of John. I think of professors like Alexander Tourginy, Theodore Wolf, John Sullivan, Edward Morton, and especially Clifford Kossel, one of the best minds ever. We also had a good man we called "Machine Gun Ferretti", who taught logic. He spoke so rapidly few besides the likes of John Navone could keep up with him.

One other passage from this Spokesman-Review column I would like to cite as indicative of Father Navone's insights: "The joy of life, at every level, is a response to the beauty of life. If we do not experience the beauty of excellence wherever we experience it, we shall never enjoy excellence wherever we find it." A passage like that is worth the price of admissions. It is a theme we find in Pope Francis, in the Evangelii Gaudium, the Joy of the Gospel. I mention Pope Francis deliberately here because, in the early days of his pontificate, in several interviews, he mentioned that, besides something of Karl Rahner, a book that most influenced him was John Navone's Theologia di Fallimento, the Theology of Failure. The notion of Pope Francis, who constantly reminds us of the joy of our faith, being struck by a discussion of "failure" reminds us that, in a sense, in this world, Christ Himself was a "failure." Belloc has a poem about it. But His failure led to what we have come to call the felix culpa, the fault that resulted in joy. This failure reminds us that, in Christianity, the redemptive suffering of the innocent Christ is the revelational addendum to the great Socratic principles that found our civilization, namely, that "it is never right to do wrong, that it is better to suffer evil than to do it."

While John Navone taught in Rome for some forty years, I was a teacher in the same University for twelve of those years. So, in addition our time together at Mt. St. Michael's, we lived in the same house in Rome, in Palazzo Frascara, during the years I was there from 1965-77. John knew Rome and many of the celebrities. He introduced me to Muriel Spark, Gore Vidal, Morris West; somehow I missed Fellini, Pasolini, Tennessee Williams, William Burrowss, and I do not know who all. He did introduce me to Father Andrew Greeley and to Francis Cardinal George.

John understood both the beauty and history of Rome. He was also Italian enough—his family was from Lucca and Genoa via Queen Anne Hill in Seattle—to know how Italian politics, social life, and business operate. This is something not so clear to us duller Midwestern types who think "cutting a deal" always verges on the shady and sinful, when it is really just a spirited, conversational way to arrive at a just price. I recall that John every so often would spot a good deal on some item at, as I recall, Antonelli's antique shop. He would purchase what he saw for his dear sister Helen in Seattle, who funded the operation, knowing her brother's good taste. Everyone recognized that John Navone could have made a fortune in the fine arts business had not the Lord sent him in another direction.

John Navone has many talents. I can recall often in Palazzo Frascara where we lived hearing him play the piano in one of the downstairs parlors. John Navone is in the enviable position of being a fine, if sometimes sharply critical, theologian of the culture. There is reason for this. To describe Father Navone as merely a "theologian" of whatever species—dogmatic, systematic, moral, historical, ascetical—is to miss the hundreds of other things that he is—a raconteur, a philosopher, a writer, an art and music critic, something of a poet, a commentator on almost everything worth commenting about. When I recall the beginnings of John's writing career back at Mt St. Michael's, I remember he once wrote an esoteric essay on something, I forget now what it was, but it was a good essay. Somehow he submitted it to a journal with the most exotic title imaginable—as I recall, The Phenomenological and Psychological Review. Much to my astonishment, but not totally as I already had begun to suspect John's many talents, they published it.

One caveat on John's talents might be mentioned. When the Gonzaga basketball team made it into the NCAA tournament this year, the Wall Street Journal sports section did a brief story on each university in the tournament. It listed four or five of the most famous alumni of the school. Under Gonzaga were, not unexpectedly, John Stockton and Tom Foley, but also listed was "Father John Navone, theologian." Needless to say, one area that seldom saw much of Navone was the sporting green. When I say that Father Navone can be sharply critical, let me cite the beginning lines of his memorable essay, "No Tradition, No Civilization":

Having lived in Europe for the last forty years, I have enjoyed the experience of historical and cultural roots. My residence for the last thirty-five years, for example, was constructed in the year that the Church of Scotland was founded, that Madrid became the capital of Spain, and the tobacco plant was imported to Western Europe by Jean Nicot. The buildings in my immediate Roman neighborhood are much older. The Colonna Palace, half a block away from my front door, was described by the Italian humanist, Petrarch (1304-74). The final 'discovery scene' of "Roman Holiday" was filmed there. Living in Europe is living in a place where the stones speak; however, if you have not done your homework, you will not understand what they are saying.

If you have no idea what a thing is, you will have a difficult time recognizing its reality when you encounter it. This principle, I suspect, is more valid of truth than beauty. For sometimes, often perhaps, we do not want to know the truth. It would require us to live differently. We protect ourselves from it by choosing not to know it. With beauty, however, we just do not see it, though sometimes we do. The beauty of what is, as Plato implied, can break into our souls almost at any time. We can only with difficulty ignore it.

II.

I came across a review by Paul Burkhard of John Navone's book *Toward a Theology of Beauty*. Let me read what Burkhard wrote: "This is an incredible book. I'm still in awe of it. It seizes your soul and takes you to the highest realms of the mind and heart of the Beautiful Triune God. I have almost an entire journal filled with notes I have taken from this book. I will look over these notes often in years to come, to let myself get swept away by the ideas present here." Burkhard goes on to mention that Navone's book does not seem to have what he calls a "progressive outline, so it is difficult to lay out everything he talks about." Anyone who reads Navone will have this similar experience of finding an amazing variety of seemingly disparate insights in everything he writes. Keeping a "Navone journal" as one reads him is not a bad idea.

I still wish I knew where he said: "We are what we remember." Memory is necessary not just to tradition but to intelligence itself. Intelligence, of course, is not memorization, however much that talent can help. But without memory, we cannot recall how things cohere. In this regard, now that both John and I have retired (I will not say "sent out to pasture"), I came across a recent scientific study. It claimed that the common feature of the members of Cicero's "On Old Age" club is that they think they are losing their memories. But this research maintains that this view is not the case. The reason the elderly, like Navone and Schall, have a tougher time remembering things is not due to a decline of memory. It is because their minds are filled with so many things that it just takes the brain, like a computer, time to find the item under consideration. Needless to say, I like this theory.

In 1998, the Roman publishing house Edizioni Dehoniane published John Navone's book Italia, natura e genio: Alle radici della cultura religioisa Italiana. This book has an English translation. (Five of Navone's books are translated into Italian—to only one of Schall's, I might add.) I came across a review in Italian of this book of John Navone by Liliana Piccinini, entitled "In risposta ai denigatori anglossoni." Navone pointed out that, among Anglo-Saxon writers at one time, there was almost a concentrated effort to downplay Italian cultural achievements. Much of this had to do with the heritage of the Reformation. But Navone directed attention to many examples of this prejudice. Writers were unwilling and unable to see the beauty and accomplishment in Italy to our civilization. Here is a rough Schall translation of Liliana Piccinini's comment about John Navone's book on Italy:

This is an original book, rich in points that lead us to reflect and certainly to an efficacious response to those who denigrate Italy. And to conclude, we should not permit ourselves to forget the book's guiding point: Rome has created "l'italianitá"—Italian-ness. There is among the Italians a common understanding almost unique in history. In Italy, the rocks also speak. At Rome, on the Campidoglio, Michaelangelo constructed his buildings with a medieval architecture that had its vaults laid on the foundations of the Romans.

As we saw earlier, John said that he lived in a place where even the stones speak. Liliana Piccinini has the Italian of this very phrase: "In Italia, parlano anche le pietre."

We are what we remember. "There is among the Italians a common understanding unique in history." The foundations of Michaelangelo's medieval buildings were built by the Romans. While in Italy, John Navone lived in a building built the same year as the Church of Scotland was founded. It was some three or four blocks from Michael's Campidoglio. Who else but John Navone would be aware of these things? "Living in Europe is living in a place where even the stones speak; however if you have not done your homework, you will not understand what they are saying." John Navone, I think, has done his homework. He listened to the stones speaking to him.

III.

Another of Father Navone's interests is statistics or "just plain facts." Every so often, I will receive from him a list of facts that causes one to think. Back in the 1970s, for example, when "population explosion" was the fad of intellectuals, I wrote a book entitled Human Dignity & Human Numbers. My argument at the time was that the world in fact had plenty of resources to feed and provide for a much larger population than the three or four billion at the time. Since that time, the issue is not population explosion, but population decline. Several writers are predicting the practical disappearance of Italians, Germans, Spanish, and other low-birth-rate people in the next decades. The only reason the United States is not on the list is because of immigration.

In any case, just recently, from out of nowhere, John Navone sent me a list of the ten most populous countries in the world in 1950, 1975, 2000, 2025, and 2050. He matter of factly noted that in 1950, three European countries, plus Russia, were in the top ten. The United States remained in the Number Three position in all the listings. But by the year 2050, India, not China, will be in the Number One position. No

European nation, including Russia, appears. The list goes: Indonesia, Nigeria, Pakistan, Brazil, Bangladesh, Ethiopia, and the Congo. This brings up the great mystery of why the West no longer wants to continue itself among the nations of the world. This mystery, as Navone hints elsewhere, happens when an individualist "rights" culture replaces one of relational responsibility to others. I mention these statistics because they are just one more sign of John Navone's curiosity about almost everything. Just how he came across them initially, I have no idea.

John Navone is often critical of Israeli military policy and of the way Hollywood pictures Christianity in a film industry that Jewish directors and owners often control or in which they have great influence. On January 11, The Economist of London, one of the world's most widely read journals, had an essay entitled "Who Is a Jew?" A couple of weeks later (January 26, 2014), The Economist published the following letter to the editor from, who else?, John Navone. It is a very interesting letter. Probably, numerically at least, more people will read this brief letter of John Navone than any of his other many publications.

The broad range of response to the question: "Who is a Jew?" opens the door to including Christians as Jews. After all, the first Christians were all Jews. They considered themselves so Jewish that the notion of baptizing gentiles was a problem for the original Jewish Christians, who believed that the Jewish Messiah had come. Amos Oz, an Israeli writer, recounts the story of his aunt's conundrum: "When the Messiah comes, we shall have to ask him whether he has been here before." The Jewish Bible is the Old Testament of the Christian Bible. Religious Jews and Christians who believe in the same God have much more in common than religious Jews and Jewish atheists. The competing answers to the question of who is a Jew suggest that the template of a fertile Jewish garden producing Orthodox, ultra-Orthodox, Reform, Christian, agnostic, and atheist Jews.

That letter is remarkably incisive; no wonder The Economist published it.

Another major theme of John Navone is that of the theology of story. This is something we associate perhaps with Tolkien, C.S. Lewis, and the writers of novels. One day I was going through something on the Internet. I came across a site entitled "Favorite Quotations Related to Story-telling." As I scroll down, whose name do I find but that of John Navone. This is what is cited:

All stories are meant to be "theological." Humankind needs theological stories because human beings are fundamentally interpersonal and because, if the Christian God's promise is true, then humankind is fundamentally related to God. God is a person. Since story is the only means by which the interpersonal reality of humankind can be expressed in its cognitive and affective fullness and since our relationship to God is fundamentally personal, it follows that story-telling and story-listening provide the most appropriate means of enabling us to live in the relationship.

Our relation to God as to one another is primarily "inter-personal." That means that it takes place at the level that is most personal, in story, in speech, in the accounts of where we have been, where we are, where we think we are going.

In a remarkably fine essay entitled "Existence as Persons In and Through Others" (Homiletic & Pastoral Review; July 6, 2013), John Navone brought together some of these themes that underlie story-telling. In it, he shows an understanding of the difference between a modern individualist "rights"-based culture, in which what is "owed" to us is central, as opposed to a gift-based culture in which the good of another is also our own concern. "We are aware of ourselves as participants in an on-going drama of existence that we did not originate, and that will continue after we are gone," Navone wrote.

We experience ourselves in sharing in a reality that is common to all, while at the same time that we are not identical. Our participation is not a matter of choice; it is simply given. So long as we are willing to regard the universe as given, in the mathematical sense of "given" which presupposes no giver, we can take existence for granted as little more than a floor for anything that is. On the other hand, we may realize that a universe of given-ness presupposes a Giver, who is generously giving them, the one originating source of all that is, the principle of unity for the universe.... The creator's free creation entails our life as a gift, not a gift which were somehow around to receive; it is we ourselves who are gift.

What follows from the notion that we ourselves are already "gifts" is that our primary mode of existence is "gratitude."

Navone sees this "gratitude" basis of our civilization as coming out of the very inner life of God which is essentially a love and otherness of persons. Created reality reflects precisely this relationship. Father Navone puts the opposite view this way:

The individualist ideal of the self-made, self-sufficient, person does not square with the reality of our relational existence. Reality is not subordinate to the human choice or wish-thought of the would-be autonomous individual. We recognize individuals and societies seriously out of touch with their relational life as delusional. We are not the product of our choices; rather our relationships are primary. Before we know who we are, we are born into a web of prior-relationships. We are related to God, Jesus Christ, our parents, relatives, and a universe before we know who we are.

The individualist, "rights"-based autonomous person makes almost any notion of sacrifice and generosity impossible.

Likewise, I would briefly like to cite yet another essay of Father Navone, one called "Aquinas' Vision of Divine and Human Happiness" (Homiletic & Pastoral Review; August 9, 2013). Human happiness, of course, is the classical Greek, eudaimonia, the "good" spirit that takes us to the highest things. Navone explains the relation of the Greek idea of happiness to the Christian transformation of it into our participation in the life of the Godhead. This discussion takes us back to the insightful classes that we had with Father Kossel on Aquinas. At the heart of Aristotle's Ethics is his treatise on friendship. It is this tractate that most naturally passes to the Christian awareness of reality when Christ, with his inner relation to the Father and the Spirit, said, at the Last Supper, "I no longer call you servants, but friends." If we realize who Christ is who says this, to whom He is related, in the same divine nature, we can see how revelation directs itself to reason as correcting and completing it.

"God is Happiness Itself, working out our sanctification as a participation in the boundless happiness of God's knowing, loving, and enjoying Himself," Father Navone writes in a beautiful passage.

We have been created by Happiness for the purpose of Happiness Itself, because God enjoys making others happy.... Our desire for happiness, the dynamic structure of human intentionality, is not of our own making; rather it evidences for Christian faith that we have been structured or preprogrammed by Happiness Itself for Happiness Itself. We are the effects of the Uncreated Cause, this Happiness Itself, which is effecting us—its will for us always being its loving self for us.

The notion that we have been personally structured for Happiness Itself is but Augustine's "restless heart."

One of the Jesuit Generals spoke of the "intellectual apostolate." This means writing, thinking, lecturing, and teaching, something to which John Navone has devoted his life. It is in a way a paradoxical life, since so much that is true is rejected as insanity, as Chesterton implied. But this life has its own rewards and pleasures, as I like to put it. In an old Peanuts, to conclude, Lucy and Charlie are out on a hillside at night, stars all about. Charlie says to her: "Do you know what I think?" As they look at the stars, Charlie continues: "I think there must be a tiny star that is out there that is MY star." Lucy looks skeptically at him as he goes on: "And as I am alone here on Earth midst millions of people, that star is out there alone midst millions and millions of stars." In the next scene, both gaze on the dark starry sky in silence. Finally, Charlie turns to Lucy to ask her: "Does that make any sense to you?" To which Lucy perkily replies: "Certainly." As she walks away to a totally deflated Charlie, she explains: "It means you're cracking up, Charlie Brown."

John Navone, for all his interests and study of things, still has time not to take himself or the world too seriously. The notion of joy and Christian humor is intrinsic to the faith. It prevents us from taking ourselves too seriously. Yet, we take ourselves seriously enough to see what Plato already saw; namely, that the only really serious thing is God whom, as John Navone explained, is, in its triune life, "Happiness Itself." That is the life that we are given as "gifts." Our only sane response to such a gift is "gratitude."

We are what we remember.

Tell me what you remember and I will tell you what you are.

About the Author:

James V. Schall, S.J. taught political philosophy at Georgetown University until recently retiring. He is the author of numerous books and countless essays on philosophy, theology, education, morality, and other topics. His most recent book is Reasonable Pleasures: The Strange Coherences of Catholicism (Ignatius Press). Visit his site, "Another Sort of Learning", for more about his writings and work.

NOTES

Preface

1. L. Orsy, S.U., "Faith and Justice: Some Reflections," in *Studies in the Spirituality of Jesuits*, Vol. VII (Sept., 1975), no. 4, p. 155.

2. B. Lonergan, *Method in Theology* (London: Darton, Longman, Todd, 1971), p. 127.

3. *Ibid.*, p. 355.

4. F. Heiler, "The History of Religions as a Preparation for the Cooperation of Religions," *The History of Religions*, M. Eliade and J. Kitagawa, eds. (Chicago: University of Chicago Press, 1959), pp. 142-153.

Chapter 1

1. R. Faricy, *Building God's World* (Denville, N.J.: Dimension Books, 1976), pp. 167f. Communism, an example of the first tendency, undercuts the value of the person. The author remarks that the individual, in this form of utopianism, has value only insofar as he is useful for the good of the collectivity. The author indicates Gnosticism as a form of the other extreme. It devaluates interpersonal relationships and charity, the bond of Christian unity.

2. J. V. Schall, "The Urgency and the Waiting," in *World Justice* 9 (1969-70) 4, p. 458. Subsequent references to this author are taken from the same page and p. 459.

Chapter 3

1. John S. Dunne, in *A Search for God in Time and Memory* (Mondon, 1967), pp. 212f., deals with the failure of Jesus' preaching in the context of the turning points in the life of Jesus which, he claims, intersected with that of John the Baptist. These points are described as the passing of night into day, as a transition from ignorance to knowledge. The first was when Jesus was baptised by John. That Jesus presented himself for a baptism of repentance suggests, for Dunne, that he was uncertain of his standing with God. His uncertainty, however, was changed into assurance as he underwent the baptism and experienced himself as beloved and pleasing to God. This left Jesus still uncertain as to whether the boundless acceptance he was receiving from God was for him alone or whether it was for others too. This unclarity was lifted at the second turning point, the imprisonment of John, when Jesus felt called upon to take John's place in proclaiming the kingdom of God. There was now a new uncertainty as to how the kingdom would come about, whether it would be effected through the conversion of Israel to God by his preaching. The third

turning point, the execution of John the Baptist, seems to lead Jesus to the belief that the kingdom would not come this way, that instead his preaching would fail and he would be executed. The fourth turning point was the darkness expressed in his death cry: "My God, my God, why have you forsaken me?" The light that followed was that of his resurrection from the dead. The experience of the previous turning points can give some foretaste of resurrection, some sense of human becoming heading toward being rather than nothingness.

Chapter 4

1. N. J. Tromp, *Primitive Conceptions of Death and the Nether World in the Old Testament* (Rome, 1969), pp. 99-128. Tromp surveys the personal aspects of Death in this section. "Mother Earth" (*Jb* 1:21) is another personification of Death. In death man returns to the nether world, his mother's womb, from whence he came (*Ps* 139:13ff.).

2. *Ibid.*, p. 100.

3. Political enemies of the king are sometimes called "evil demons." See S. Mowinckel, *The Psalms in Israel's Worship* (Oxford, 1962), vol. 1, p. 200.

4. M. Eliade, *The Myth of the Eternal Return*, tr. from the French by W. Trask, Bollingen Series XLVI (Princeton, 1965), pp. 39-162. This fourth chapter is entitled "The Terror of History."

5. Job had been troubled by the proximity of death because it deprived him of the opportunity of coming to terms with God within his time; Jesus, on the other hand, accepts God's time for his death, despite the fact that his preaching has not yet succeeded in converting his people.

6. This quote is taken from H. de la Costa, S.J., "Liberation of All Man: Our Common Objective," a conference given at the VI Assembly of the General Council of the World Federation of Christian Life Communities, Augsburg, Germany, Aug. 4-10, 1973. Pamphlet, *Supplement to Progressio* (Rome, 1973), p. 21.

7. G. H. P. Thompson, *The Gospel According to Luke* (Oxford, 1972), p. 29.

8. Failure, as missing the mark and falling short of expectation, is synonymous with sin. It is linked with death and Satan. It is that abiding sense of failing to measure up to ideals, of failing to find the meaning, goal, and purpose of life or to be in harmony with God, neighbour and self (cf. *Pr* 8:35). It is the failure to accept dependence upon God. The sinner decides to be the ultimate principle of his own life, no longer acknowledging that it is God and not himself who has made him what he is. In sin man turns from the ultimate source of his true life and toward himself (*Col* 1:21; *Ep* 4:14). Through sin, death entered the world (*Rm* 5:12) when the first man sundered harmonious relations with God for the entire race. Underlying Paul's affirmation is the traditional Old Testament belief that sin brings death; because all men die, he concludes that all men are sinners, even if they have not sinned personally.

9. V. Taylor, *The Names of Jesus* (London, 1954).

10. J. Mitros, "Patristic Views of Christ's Salvific Work," in *Thought*, Autumn 1967, p. 444.

Chapter 5

1. K. Rahner and H. Vorgrimler, "Temptation," in *Theological Dictionary*

(New York: Herder & Herder, 1965), p. 454.

2. See John Navone, "Satan Returns," in *The Furrow*, 26 (September 1975), 9, pp. 541-50.

3. John L. McKenzie, *Dictionary of the Bible* (Milwaukee: Bruce, 1965), art. "Temptation," p. 878.

4. Bernard Lonergan, *Method in Theology* (London: Darton, Longman and Todd, 1971), pp. 242f.

5. *Ibid.*, p. 243.

6. *Ibid.*, p. 244.

7. *Ibid.*

8. *Early Christian Writings*, tr. M. Staniforth (Baltimore: Penguin Books, 1968), P.277.

9. B. Tyrrell S.J., *Christotherapy* (New York: Seabury Press, 1975), pp. 87-96.

10. S. Hauerwas, "The Significance of Vision," in *Studies in Religion*, vol. 2 (Summer 1972), 1, p. 36.

11. B. Lonergan, *Method in Theology*, p. 117.

12. John Sheets S.J., "Your Adversary," in *The Way* 2 (January 1962), 1, p. 43.

13. Bernard Cooke, "The Hour of Temptation," in *The Way* 2 (July 1962), 3, p. 179.

14. T. W. Manson, *The Mission and Message of Jesus*, p. 337.

15. John Sheets S.J., "Your Adversary," in *The Way* 2 (January 1962), 1, p. 41.

16. Gerard Hughes S.J., "Renouncing the World," in *The Way* 2 (January 1962), 1, p. 49.

17. Gerard Hughes, *op. cit.*, p. 50.

Chapter 6

1. P. L. Berger and John Neuhaus, *Movement and Revolution* (Garden City, N.Y.: Doubleday Anchor Books, 1970), p. 19.

2. *Ibid.*

3. P. L. Berger and John Neuhaus, *Movement and Revolution* (Garden City, N.Y.: Doubleday Anchor Books, 1970), pp. 184-186.

4. L. Orsy, S.J., "Faith and Justice," in *Studies in the Spirituality of Jesuits*, Vol. VII (September, 1975) 4, pp. 163-164.

5. J. V. Schall, S.J., "Ethics and International Affairs," in *World Justice*, Vol. 6, No. 4 (June, 1965), p. 472.

6. B. Sorge, "Violence in Social and Political Groups," Vatican radio interview, in *SJ Press and Information Office Documentation*, No. 19 (Nov. 21, 1973, P. 3).

7. *Ibid.*

Chapter 7

1. R. Niebuhr, "The Diversity and Unity of History," reprinted in *The Philosophy of History in Our Time*, ed. H. Meyerhoff (New York, 1959), p. 317.

2. H. Meyerhoff, *The Philosophy of History in Our Time,* p. 9.

3. *Ibid.,* p. 8.

4. *Ibid.,* p. 9.

5. K. Popper, "Has History Any Meaning?" *ibid.,* p. 305.

6. *Ibid.,* p. 307.

7. G. von Rad, *The Message of the Prophets,* tr. by D. M. G. Stalker (London, 1968), p. 273.

8. *Ibid.*

9. H. Wheeler Robinson, *Inspiration and Revelation in the Old Testament* (Oxford, 1946), p. 132.

Chapter 8

1. R. Woods (Boston, 1898). The theatre of the absurd gives eloquent expression to man's experience of the wilderness condition: Albee, Adamov, Arrabal, Beckett, Genet, Ionesco. The existentialists Camus and Satre do the same.

2. N. Algren (New York, 1960). Arthur Miller's *Death of a Salesman* employs considerable wilderness imagery to express the perils of life in modern society.

3. J. Gottmann, *Megalopolis* (New York, 1961), p. 216.

4. Lucretius spoke for his age in *De Rerum Natura.* He observed that it was a serious defect that so much of the earth was possessed of wilderness full of restless dread. He describes this as the context of pre-civilised life, where man lived a nightmarish existence, hounded by dangers on all sides. He relates how man escaped his miserable wilderness condition through the development of his intelligence and inventions.

5. There were other elements basic to man's hostility and terror of the wilderness. Many folk traditions associate the wilderness with the supernatural and monstrous. It had a quality of mystery that triggered the imagination. To frightened eyes the limbs of trees became grotseque, leaping figures, and the wind sounded like a weird scream. The wild forest seemed animated with fantastic creatures lurking in its depths. Whether propitiated with sacrifices as deities or regarded as devils, these forest beings were feared. See A. Porteus, *Forest Folklore, Mythology, and Romance* (New York, 1928).

6. Pan, lord of the woods in classical mythology, had the legs, ears, and tail of a goat and the body of a man. He combined gross sensuality with boundless energy. Greeks passing through forests dreaded an encounter with Pan. The word "panic" originated from the blinding fear that seized travellers upon hearing strange cries in the wilderness and assuming them to signify Pan's approach.

7. R. Funk, "The Wilderness," in *Journal of Biblical Literature* 78 (1959), pp. 205-214.

8. J. Navone, *Themes of St. Luke* (Rome, 1970), pp. 170-179.

9. Almost everywhere the expulsion of demons, diseases, and sins coincides, or at one period coincided, with the festival of the New Year, celebrating the resumption of time from the beginning in a passage from chaos to cosmos. Such exorcisms effect a kind of new creation.

10. F. Crowe "Salvation as Wholeness," in *Canadian Journal of Theology* 14 (1968), p. 234.

11. Speculative theology and philosophic efforts to reach God are not immediately relevant to the stimulation of religious feeling, but if one's knowledge of God's existence and one's imperfect understanding of one's faith are to be operative in spontaneity they must be linked with symbols that engage one's sensitivity. Prayer is such a symbol. It is a sensitive engagement of the psyche associated with one's knowledge and belief.

12. B. Lonergan, *Method in Theology* (London, 1971), pp. 64-69.

13. P. Ricoeur, *The Symbolism of Evil* (Boston, 1967), p. 351. Through critical interpretation, aided by the insights of all the sciences, religious symbols regain their power to transmit the sacred. We must understand to believe, and we must believe to understand fully.

14. E. Erikson, in "The Development of Ritualization." *The World Year Book of Religion*, Vol. 1 (London, 1969), p. 712, maintains that ritualisation is essential for human development: separateness transcended and distinctiveness confirmed in the mutuality of recognition. The wilderness condition is dehumanising for its lack of authentic community with God and man; it is devoid of that ritualisation which characterises authentically human relationships with God and man.

15. See R. Rousseau, "Secular and Christian Images of Man," in *Thought* 47 (1972), pp. 167-200.

Chapter 9

1. God remembers certain persons and shows them his grace and mercy (*Gn* 8:1; 19:29; 30:22; *Ex* 32:13; 1 *S* 1:11, 19; 25:31). His remembering is an efficacious and creative event, which enables man to remember God.

2. Deuteronomy especially develops a theology of remembering (*Dt* 5:15; 7:18; 8:2, 18; 9:7; 15:15; 16:3, 12; 24:18, 20, 22; 32:7). Israel should especially remember its trials in Egypt (*Dt* 15:15; 16:12; 24:18, 20, 22) and should learn a new obedience and trust from them and avoid disobedience and arrogance.

3. The importance of the future is studied by N. Cohn in *The Pursuit of the Millennium: Revolutionary Messianism in Medieval and Reformation Europe and Its Bearing on Modern Totalitarian Movements* (New York, 1961). If we believe that the future of an act (the images, visions, heavens, and all forms of perfect commonwealth) determines, along with the past, how we act in the present, then we ought to study visions of the future, as we do those in which we "recapture" the past. As Mannheim made clear, a utopian as much as a conservative style of thought affects how we act. And as Dewey and Mead taught, we envision a future to make action in a present possible. Although each present has its future, there are few histories of these futures. Cohn's book indicates how much could be gained from the study of future visions of ideal societies.

4. N. D. O'Donoghue, in "Space and Time as Ethical Categories," *Continuum* 6 (1968), p. 164, affirms that man is memory as well as intentionality, and as memory he dominates time and change. Man's permanence, unlike that of a stone, involves a living grasp and assimilation of the flow of experience. Memory assimilates what time has devoured and transforms it, holding and preserving it within the light of another world. Memory is more than a mirror of experience or a record of the past; it is active and constructive, giving new significance to the present in fitting it into the pattern of the past and reinterpreting the past in the light of each succeeding present. Memory seeks ever greater fulfilment, but it seeks it without anxiety, waiting for the future without losing anything

of the past. O'Donoghue admits hat man loses the past in its sharp actuality, for memory is not the whole of man, but insofar as man is memory he cuts across the temporal flow and dominates it. Memory opens up the possibility of the mutual involvement of past, present, and future. All time is eternally present. Man's domination of experience and therefore his responsibility covers the past, present and future; the past is not only what I have done but what I do with it now as it lives in my memory, if only by recognising it as what it is.

5. My article, "Memories Make the Future," from *The Catholic World* (Dec. 1966, pp. 149-153), contains material which illuminates the role of remembering both in perpetuating and in overcoming human failure. Parts of that article are reprinted and slightly readapted here.

Chapter 10

1. C. K. Barrett, *The Holy Spirit and the Gospel Tradition* (London, 1947), p. 23. The new life of the redeemed Israel is God's life because it results from his creative Spirit. In both creations the Spirit is *Creator Spiritus*.

2. L. Legrand, "L'arrière-plan néotestamentaire de Lc. I, 35," *Revue Biblique* 70 (1963), p. 164.

3. H. von Baer, *Der Heilige Geist in den Lukasschriften* (Stuttgart, 1926), pp. 59f.

4. J. Dupont, "Filius meus es tu, L'interpretation de Ps., ii, 7 dans le Nouveau Testament," in *Revue des Sciences Religieuses* 35 (1948), p. 522.

5. G. W. H. Lampe, "The Holy Spirit in the Writings of St Luke," in *Studies in the Gospels: Essays in Memory of R. R. Lightfoot*, ed. D. E. Nineham (Oxford, 1953), p. 170.

6. G. H. P. Thompson, *The Gospel according to Luke* (Oxford, 1972), p. 29.

7. J. Jeremias, *The Central Message of the New Testament* (London, 1965), p. 30.

8. See A. Richardson, *The Miracle-Stories of the Gospels* (London, 1941).

9. See E. Andrews, "Gifts of Healing," in *The Interpreter's Dictionary of the Bible*, Vol. 2 (New York, 1962), p. 548.

10. J. Jeremias, *The Central Message of the New Testament, op. cit.*, p. 29.

11. See A. B. Du Toit, *Der Aspekt der Freude im urchristlichen Abendmahl* (Winterthur, 1965). Also, J. Navone, *Themes of St Luke* (Rome, 1970), where the seventh chapter is on the theme of joy.

12. P. Baelz, *Prayer and Providence* (London, 1968), p. 131.

13. K. Hemmerle, "Evil," in *Sacramentum Mundi*, Vol. 2 (London, 1968), p. 282.

14. J. Macquarrie, *Principles of Christian Theology* (London, 1966), p. 282.

15. *Ibid.*, p. 238.

16. G. W. H. Lampe, "The Holy Spirit in the Writings of St Luke," *op. cit.*, p. 170.

17. See B. Lonergan, *Method in Theology* (London, 1972), p. 118. Lonergan explains that conversion is a lifelong process. It is also a change of direction (p. 52).

18. John Macquarrie, *Principle of Christian Theology, op. cit.*, p. 358.

19. B. Lonergan, *Method in Theology, op. cit.*, p. 109, cites common elements of religious experience in major world religions, distinguished by F. Heiler's

"The History of Religions as a Preparation for the Cooperation of Religions," in *The History of Religions*, ed. by M. Eliade and J. Kitagawa (Chicago, 1959), pp. 142-53. See also Lonergan's resume of this material in the xeroxed copy of his lecture, "The Future of Christianity," Holy Cross College, Worcester, Mass., 1969, pp. 1-3.

20. Related articles of Dr Thomas Hora that bear upon the material covered here: "Cognition and Health," *The Journal of Religion and Health* I, No. 3 (April 1962); "Beyond Self," *Psychologia* V, No. 2 (June 1962); "The Transpersonal Perspective," *The American Journal of Psychoanalysis* 23, No. 1 (May 1963); "Responsibility," *Review of Existential Psychology and Psychiatry* II, No. 3 (Fall 1962); "The Epistemology of Love," *Journal of Existential Psychiatry* II, No. 7 (Winter 1962).

Mike Hamms
P. 42 - The kind of person His Father
wanted Him to be

Made in the USA
Lexington, KY
10 May 2016